Not

So

Politically

Correct

John S. Davies

Warning! There may be locker room language inside these pages

Not

So

Politically

Correct

ISBN-13:

978-1548662134

ISBN-10:
1548662135

JDF Publications

c/o The JDavies Company
2220 Otay Lakes Rd. Suite #502-211
Chula Vista, CA 91915

First printing 2017

Cover art:
specialforcesartdepartment.com

INTRODUCTION

We just ferociously battled through one of the most contentious political campaigns ever for the office of the President of the United States. We now have a new leader and he is an outsider. That doesn't happen.

This outsider caused a lot of commotion. In his campaign he revealed the underbelly of American politics and its financiers. As unpleasant as it was, we needed it. We needed the truth to come out. We now must take a long and in depth look at our thoughts and behaviors.

We should look at this both seriously and humorously. If we only look at it seriously we will end up spending all our money on therapy. So don't hesitant to find the humor in this system we now know is totally f*cked up but it is ours.

Not

So

Politically

Correct

This page is reserved for reviews. I will list them once I finish them.

CNN reported one of their anchors, they won't reveal who, was just attended to by paramedics after tripping over a fact. CNN refuses to admit it was a fact despite it walking, talking and looking like a fact. Others are bewildered as to how a fact made it into the CNN studio despite giving security explicit instructions not to allow any facts into the building. The world is still waiting for a tweet response from President Trump.

The only reason governments around the world try desperately to sanitize each episode of murderous rampage as not related to Islamic terror is because they would have to admit they can't control it.

If the Puerto Ricans are holding a parade in New York honoring a terrorist who set off more than 100 bombs in the USA, why the hell would we want Puerto Rico to be the 51st state? After that ISIS will want to be the 52nd state. Before you know it we will have 57 states.

We keep seeing pictures of Vladimir Putin whispering in Hillary Clinton's ear. Putin doesn't speak English and Hillary doesn't speak Russian. Hmm.

European progressives allowed a frumpy old woman in the form of Angela Merkel (a minion of the EU) to dramatically alter the composition of Germany and its neighbors in a way that will be forever mourned.

The irony is too much. While Miami Dolphin players chose to disrespect America by taking a knee during the National Anthem, in front of them standling proudly was a United States Marine, the first in battle, to protect the right of these morons to do this.

Doctors realized Hillary Clinton had a cardio problem and attempted to implant a pacemaker but couldn't find a heart.

Snoop Dogg, a product of white billionaires, says white billionaire Donald Trump is a "reckless mother f*cker." A loud WTF to the white billionaires who created this Dogg turd.

North Korea is now threatening to bomb New York which is 11000 miles from North Korea. Since Kim Jong-un doesn't have a missile that can travel more then 2500 miles there will have to be four layovers on the way. He is arranging to do the layovers on Chinese built islands.

Authorities are currently trying to locate anyone who cares what Nancy Pelosi thinks. So far no one has been found.

Terrorism, murder, sex crimes and the drug trade are serious problems in America but thanks to the "new" America we are more focused on the words we use or the chalk outlines on a college campus.

Every time the democrats reach into Trump's closet and pull out a skeleton that they think is damaging evidence against him, it backfires. Bigly.

As a business you can refuse service to a person lawfully carrying a gun or a cop who wants a cake that says Blue Lives Matter and they can do nothing about it, but if a business refuses a wedding cake to gay guys, they can be sued for hundreds of thousands of dollars.

Pakistan is threatening to nuke India. Iran wants to nuke Israel. North Korea is threatening to nuke everybody. This is what happens when the world lacks a leader. America needs to lead again.

There is at least one thing we all should like Donald Trump for. He exposed both the republican and democrat morons who behave like children and can't be trusted while continuing to collect a paycheck from the taxpayer. For that we should be grateful to Trump.

NBA center for the Knicks Joakim Noah skipped a team dinner at West Point Military Academy because he has "mixed feelings and is against war." It's probably a good thing because we don't want our up and coming warriors to catch anything like the stupidity Noah suffers from.

According to sources, Paul Ryan and Luis Gutierrez have become engaged.

Liberals just won't accept the f*cked up mess we call the refugee crisis. Despite it being an obvious and dangerous situation both physically as well as financially, they are pushing their political belief that you must extend a hand before all else. It doesn't matter how often or how deeply that hand is biten, they are going to extend it.

If you are a liberal you think it is okay that an 8 year old little boy thinks he's a girl and his parents encourage it. There's something wrong here folks. Wake up and smell the stupidity.

To Hillary we are deplorable, to Obama we are crude. To Trump we are American.

When two women were arrested for having sex with a 15 year old boy at a pizza party the only question the liberals had was what kind of pizza?

Bruce Springsteen was rushed to the hospital today suffering from guilt as a result of White Privilege. He trashes his white fans, who made him who he is, to assuage his quilt but it wasn't enough so he is now a spokesman for the #blacklivesmatter movement which pleases his 3 black fans.

The Elites, and you know who you are, see no problem with immigration and refugees coming to America. That is because the last contact Elites had with our world was...let me think...never!

If you are one of the 95 million workers not in the workforce any longer, you don't think favorably about others being brought into America to work.

If you want to constantly live in the shadow of terrorism, if you are okay with cops getting beat up or killed, if you want to worry that you may never get a job while foreigners do, if you want your daughter going to the bathroom with boys, if you want to keep paying more taxes to support illegals and refugees, if you want race riots in America's streets, if you want to live with the threat of nuclear war, by all means vote Democrat.

Political science is free to learn online.

CNN aka Clinton News Network aka Chicano News Network aka Crappy News Network aka Corrupt News Network has finally admitted being a shill for democrats. The evidence is overwhelming.

The liberals are condemning Trump for tweeting while still letting Middle Easterners on visas with names no American can pronounce, take flight lessons in America. One of them just crashed a plane in a downtown Connecticut city.

I don't see the attraction in a girl's butt as big as a liquor store. You know the butt I'm talking about. Is it so you can find it in the dark?

For all those who have underdeveloped brain mass, the NYTimes attacks on Trump is Mexico attacking Trump because the major stockholder is Carlos Slim the richest man in Mexico.

Paris now looks like the worst slum known to mankind after being inundated by refugees from Africa. The European version of the progressive media is blaming French citizens for improperly welcoming the refugees.

I worked hard all my life, retired from law enforcement, but I'm a white guy that supports Trump so I guess, according to liberals, I'm a piece of shit. Go figure! I had no idea.

A liberal judge in Montana gave a guy that raped his 12 year old daughter a suspended sentence of 30 years. The incestual rapist only did 17 days in jail. Is this what we want in America's future? Liberal thinking like this?

Congressional aides have reported the village idiot has escaped. Officials are frantically trying to locate Eddie Munster aka Rep. Paul Ryan. One tip places him on Rep. Luis Gutierrez's lap.

Refugees are a package deal. You get get the grossly undereducated, the culture, the religion, dependency, diseases, hatred, and for Democrats you get the vote.

It's pretty scary when you realize a lot of us are smarter than the politicians asking for our vote. I'm just saying, when you hear what comes out of them and read what they write, it dawns on you that these are not rocket scientists. I actually do want the person who is representing me to be smarter than me.

Why is the NYDaily News still reporting on politics? That's like PETA reporting on how to properly skin a bear. Stick with what you know, gossip.

Rosie O'Donnell was heard screaming obscenities from her home at 123 The Gutter On the Left Ave. Grossville, USA. Enough already, the election is over.

For the sake of argument lets agree that all politicians are immoral idiots. Now we can discuss which idiot is better, this way we are forced to actually look at the issues. The differences in issues are stark. Make your decision based on issues. It's that simple.

The one important thing mass migration advocates don't talk about is how the immigrants prefer to have multiple wives and as many as 20 children. That means one immigrant male equals up to 20-30 people in total.

Not a good idea to f*ck with Russia since Hillary made it possible for them to get a boatload of uranium from us.

The police responded to a call from a local motel about loud words indentified as stupid shit. Joy Behar and Bill Kristol were subsequently arrested for disturbing everyone's peace.

Democrat Sheila Jackson Lee after denouncing Wikipedia went on to denounce the validity of an I.Q. Test.

The democrats, a group not known for their honesty, would have you think there is only about twelve women left in the United States that haven't accused Donald Trump of sexual assault. Yesterday, Paul Ryan claimed Trump grabbed his ass. That would make it eleven women left.

In real estate the mantra is location, location, location. In politics the mantra is issues, issues, issues. Every politician has a closet packed full of skeletons, keep your eye on the issues. That's what counts in the end.

Hillary Clinton made a speech on poverty while wearing a jacket that cost $12,700.00

Polling is about as accurate as a government report or a suicide bomber or a ballistic missile fired by North Korea.

Ronald Reagan is turning over in his grave because of the behavior of the Republican Elites.

Obama has filed papers for a name change changing his name to Barack Alinsky.

Bob Schieffer, speaking from the cafeteria of a rest home, said he talked to twelve republicans who say they think Trump could lose because of his lewd remarks. Bob Schieffer hasn't talked to twelve republicans in his entire life.

Another couple of women have come forward and claim Donald Trump was crude with them. The dates they say it happened was before he was born. The democrats need to use a f*cking calendar.

All of a sudden the liberals, who are all about T&A, are behaving like they have reserved seats in the Church of the Righteous.

It is rumored Kim Kardashian, a Hillary supporter, thinks Donald Trump is lewd. No one knows where the pot and the kettle were when she said this.

Even when you think Congress is in session, they aren't since there is not a noticable difference unless you count the number of people in their private restaurants.

The White House can't find Air force One. It landed with Obama in America's 57th state.

Remember, George H.W. Bush is why we got Bill Clinton and George W. Bush is why we got Barack Obama. This is why you shouldn't listen to the Bush family. Their failures have hurt us tremendously.

Miley Cyrus while on stage performing, encouraged young fans to touch her pussy (and they did) yet she condemned Trump for saying the word pussy. She's so dumb she probably can't spell double standard.

I asked the registrar of voters if I can vote multiple times since dead people can.

When an actor speaks without a script it is obvious why they have scripts.

"Banging" Bill Clinton has a new accuser to add to the long list of women who have "darkened his door." Tonight the Association of Locker Room Attendants is presenting him an award for his unending efforts to get women in bed. Clinton is a hero among men who spend time in locker rooms.

A prominent republican from the George W. Bush Administration said if Trump wins it will be the end of the republican brand. Even a 5th grader knows the republican brand ended with the election of G.W. Bush.

You can take all the video footage from the 2016 campaign for president and make a Emmy winning comedy series out of it. It's hilarious.

America was hit with some very bad news today. The Obamas and the Bidens said they will stay in Washington after leaving office and will stay "involved." Just when you thought it was safe to go back in the water.

In a speech today Obama went to blame someone else for whatever he was talking about and had to pull a list out of his pocket to refer to. He went down the list until he got to the Girl Scouts of America.

Washington D.C. is now rated the stinkiest town in America. With the mass media pulling story after story out of their asses, the town has gone up in stink.

In 2013 President Obama took a vacation of four days to golf with Tiger Woods in Florida. It cost the taxpayer 3.6 million dollars. I wonder how many veterans died in Florida during those four days because Obama ignored them?

Calling the Republican Congress a loose knit group would be a compliment. They are more like a bunch of dirty bastards. They can't even be trusted around their own mothers. If you look up POS in the dictionary you will see a group picture of them. They are starting to make the democrats look credible.

Bill and Hillary Clinton are the Bonnie and Clyde of politics.

Liberals are America's most fearsome enemy. They are willing to let our nation take a hit for their own gain.

Hillary showed up at the White House and demanded her rightful place in the Oval Office. The security guard refused entry.

CNN's Brian Stelter, who still has a wedgie from high school, had the gall to say the resignation of National Security Advisor Mike Flynn was due to investigative journalism. Stelter, who was rumored to have served in the Cub Scouts, knows full well it was an Obama operative who still works at the White House and hasn't been fired yet.

When Senator Al Franken (I still can't believe he is a senator) was late for work an aide was dispatched to his house where he found the senator in the closet under a pile of skeletons.

Tick tock, tick tock, when are the republicans going to show their faces in support of our republican president? We're waiting.

Did Obama stack the intelligence community the past eight years? Are we seeing the result of that now? You are a moron if you put anything past Barack Obama. He is a Chicago politician.

The liberal political force, albeit a failure, that is disrupting the lives of Americans has been allowed to grow in strength for eight years without any resistance from republicans. This disaster is on republicans. These republicans don't give a shit because they are bunch of little bitches that didn't like that an outsider came in and took their presidency. A bunch of white boys with no balls bought and paid for by wealthy donors. And I am a white conservative so these punks can't fool me.

If the left wants to blow everything out of proportion, start sending the Secret Service after those who threaten the life of the President of the United States.

Look what the busting of a dam in California has revealed. The democratic super majority in California spends 25 billion dollars a year on illegals and they decided to spend zero on fixing the dam in Oroville, CA. Don't be mistaken, the 25 billion dollars wasn't spent out of the goodness of their hearts, it was spent to create the super majority they now have. The price of political power.

What can be said about republicans not coming to the defense of their newly minted republican president under siege by a low life democrat party of sore losers? As a loyal conservative it pains me greatly that the party of conservatives now behave like liberals. It is time for a third party.

President Trump has done his level best to appease the establishment traitors, I mean the republicans, by having Mike Pence as his VP, Reince Priebus as his COS, Sean Spicer as his PS, and of course, Elaine Chao as a Cabinet member. The thanks he gets is a set of steak knives implanted in his back.

Clinton News Network's Jake "I'm a wuss" Tapper plagiarized a line that millions used for eight years with Obama. "Get to work and stop whining about it" was what Obama was told almost daily as he trashed America here and abroad and almost always from a golf course.

If the republicans would remove the sticks from their collective asses and get on the Trump Train it would catapult the brand into the stratosphere. Popularity and the number of new member sign-ups would soar. But that would mean listening to the people. Hmm.

Archeologists stumbled upon what they thought was the oldest piece of fossilized crap ever discovered in modern history. As it turns out it was simply Senate Majority leader Mitch McConnell taking a nap.

A liberal's hate must run deep if they feel they have to attack a 10 year old Baron Trump to make their point. Disgusting.

Happening Now: not sure this is real or fake news but it is being said that Obama tripped over a prayer rug while trying to make a donation at his mosque.

Democrats are raising questions about Donald Trump's mental health. Am I missing something here? A democrat is raising a question about someone's mental health? How ironic.

Those who make the best argument for legal immigration are those who came here legally. They earned their life in America by following the rules.

Based on the behaviors we see today all over the globe, the term conspiracy theory will drop from use. It's all real.

All it would take to fix Brain Stelter of the Clinton News Network is hair plugs, a low carb diet, a pair of testicles and a brain implant. Then he could go to work for a real news network.

If you are not quite sure what fake news is just read the dailymail.com. It is chock full of fake news especially about Trump. The hatred for Trump screams at you when you read the news on their site. I go to that site and other liberal sites so as a conservative I am not accused of not knowing how the liberals think.

All you have to know about Sweden and its lame refusal to admit is has an immigrant problem is that they have no-go zones. Enough said.

I'm don't know why so many people are complaining about California's crappy infrastructure. Sure, the state is crumbling beneath our feet and your car is a pothole away from a major mechanical repair, but look at the fantastic way we take care of our illegals! And now we can do the same for refugees. How many states do you know of that provide $25 billion a year to the cause of these people? And believe me, the California liberals have made it their only cause.

Barack Hussein Obama, your turn is over. Have some dignity towards the country that so graciously granted you an opportunity of a lifetime. Ride off into the sunset, please.

Before Trump even figured out where the toilet was in the White House liberals were condemning his presidency.

Rep. Maxine Waters (D-Stupidville) went on MSNBC and said Trump's Cabinet picks "are a bunch of scumbags." She is an elected politician. Chew on that for awhile. That means voters went to the polls and thought "this woman is someone I want in Congress representing America."

Since ObamaCare is simply an expansion of the existing Medicaid program how hard could it be to shit can it?

To Bruce Jenner: Look what you and your family has given the world. We don't need your advice. We are better off without it.

House Speaker Paul Ryan aka Eddie Munster took a staged tour of the border put on by Border Patrol management and was heard exclaiming "OMG so that's what a border looks like."

The democrats have elected Tom Perez and Keith Ellison as Chair and Co-Chair of the Democratic National Committee. The DNC is aware they didn't get the support they needed from the Hispanic and Muslim communities so they are resorting to pimping. It is so their style.

Has anyone seen Senator Mitch McConnell and Representative Paul Ryan? These two pieces of garbage are huddling somewhere with Senator Lindsey Graham and Senator John McCain to fine tune their strategy to derail the Trump train. We would be better off if the Trump train ran over these assholes.

George Clooney, a man about the world, defends every country except America. Without America, who would George Clooney be?

This morning Iran, like China, is rattling their sabers to see if Trump is going to continue an eight year Obama foreign policy of rope-a-dope.

If the commissioner of the New York Police Department is telling his officers to disregard Trump's immigration mandate, how are we suppose to support cops? If cops in New York go against the President of the United States who is going to do great things for them after Obama trashed them and caused so many to lose their lives to BLM thugs, what are we suppose to do? This is a Police Commissioner who is being manipulated by Mayor of New York Bill de Bullshit and doesn't have the nuts to stand up to him.

In a fit of anger today Bernie Sanders admonished Americans by saying if they had voted for him they wuold have a lot free shit by now.

To all the stupid followers of liberals: The actors and rock stars and politicians and fat cats all live where you don't. They don't come to your house or invite you to their house. They don't pay your bills and they are not their when your child is sick. And yet you follow them like they are your best friend. When was the last time you answered your phone and it was Katy Perry or Madonna or George Clooney? Get a grip on your reality. These people don't live in our reality.

Is anyone in Congress working? The democrats are using their time to trash Trump and the republicans are hiding from Trump in the basements of the 1%. No one is working except Trump!

"Neanderthal DNA Still Affects Health and Looks of Modern Humans" was the headline of an article this morning. Duh. Tell us something we don't know. They have been rioting in the streets since the beginning of the 2016 presidential election and haven't stopped yet. They work for the democrats. Just check their pay stubs.

Bingo! We have a winner. It appears Senator Tom Cotton (R-Badass) is going to be a republican that utilizes his testicles and not cower and hide in the Senate bathroom like most of his colleagues.

We are awaiting today's victim of Hillary's wrath over her loss. It could have been her. Just sayin'.

New DNC Chair Tom Perez has stated Trump has "proposed nothing but chaos and carnage." Having been Barack Obama's Secretary of Labor Mr. Perez would surely recognize chaos and carnage having viewed it from a front row seat for the last eight years.

There is obviously two Americas 1) the America where the mass media, celebrities, politicians, freeloaders and billionaires reside and 2) the America where working men and women reside and make it possible for the folks named in the first America to have what they have.

As a white male I had no idea I was responsible for all that is wrong in the world. Shame on me.

Bad guys, bad guys, bad guys. This is what we need to go after. If they are here in the form of an illegal then so be it. They must go.

In Jackson, MS a severed head was found on a porch. Police said the cause of death is probably severance. For all they know the man's body could be walking around looking for its head. Geez, these are the police who will investigate this murder.

The effects of the ongoing battle against ISIS is starting to show now that Trump has given the okay for our warriors to be warriors. ISIS is now down to ISI.

The problem Trump is dealing with in Washington is he simply doesn't understand Swamp Etiquette. Once he learns that from the republican and democrat Swamp dwellers, he will be fine. He should talk with Lindsey Graham, he wrote the book Swamp Etiquette For Everyday Use, it is co-authored by John McCain.

Hillary Clinton emerged from her rabbit hole to urge Trump to come out against hate crimes. He has. He just canceled his appearance at the Correspondents Dinner. The mass media is committing hate crimes against our president daily.

We saw Paul Ryan (R-Traitorville) last week on a horse. This week we see him sitting in a gym pumping iron. I guess next we will see him cuddling a brown bear. He is America's version of Vladimir Putin.

Sen. Bernie Sanders (D-Woodstock) appeared at President Trump's first speech before a joint session of Congress bedecked in a suit by designer "Frumpy."

Now Sen. Elizabeth Warren (D-Cuckoo) is saying she dated Geronimo.

Rumor has it that former president Barack Obama had a teleprompter set up in his living room so he could talk to his family.

It can't get any more pathetic than having Rep. Maxine Waters as your spokesperson.

The White House is reporting an individual was found in Des Moines, Iowa who did not meet with the Russian Ambassador. That brings the count of the number of people who did not meet with the Ambassador to one.

Valerie Jarrett, resurrected as a one-woman goon squad for former president Obama, said the Obama White House never interfered with an independent investigation by the Department of Justice. That's like Bill Clinton saying he never interfered with the decisions made by his dick.

I have spoken with the Russian Ambassador and he will be coming over for dinner tonight. It was easy, all I had to do was send a text.

Those concerned are still investigating the whereabouts of republican elites who have been conspicuously absent while crazed democrats attack our republican president. Sources who refuse to be named say they are huddled in the conference room of the Benedict Arnold Association for Asshole Traitors aka Sen. Lindsey Graham's living room.

Sen. Ben Sasse was found this morning sharing a pair of boxer shorts with Sen. Lindsey Graham. More on this later.

Despite overwhelming evidence that the democrats have conducted a campaign of deceit, the democrats demand overwhelming overwhelming evidence.

The Democratic National Committee is requiring all registered democrats to attend Facts 101. It is a class taught by republicans to address the correlation between facts and the truth. Obviously grading will be on a curve based on the realization the material is new to the democrats. Fees for the class will be paid in Russian Rubles which is the democrats favored currency.

It was rumored today that a republican was seen working. No verification yet.

The 500,000 illegals New York Mayor Bill De Bullshit has sworn to hide, were found. They were in a spare bedroom at the official residence of the Mayor. It seems they all work for him.

There is a rumor that the Democrats "anonymous sources" were seen having lunch today with Nancy Pelosi. It turns out it was just Barack Obama. Wait...you don't think...no it couldn't be.

Louis Farrakhan, leader of the Nation of Islam and one of America's most well-known morons, said "America is the most rotten nation on earth." Then f*cking leave, turd.

When Mexicans can't stand Mexico anymore they leave for the United States. When Americans say they can't stand America anymore they don't go anywhere.

Rep. Paul Ryan (R-Turncoat) was seen shopping for steak knives at Macy's. He favors the plunging style.

Sen. Lindsey Graham (R-Turncoat) was rumored to have joined the A Day Without A Woman march. Need I explain why?

Linda Sarsour, hero to democrat women, openly supports Sharia Law and almost always flashes the sign of ISIS when interviewed. That alone should cause an investigation.

Next stop for douchebag Keith Olbermann is well...there is no next stop. He is already at the bottom.

How would you like to be at a train station or an airport and all of a sudden a man with an axe comes barreling through trying to hack people to death. This is occurring now in Europe and you better hope it doesn't happen in America.

"Taxpayers funded eight nonprofits that serve, protect or advocate for illegal immigrants with more than $291 million between 2012 to 2016." A headline this morning that might interest you.

Hillary popped up again today kinda like a gopher pops up out of his hole on a golf course. She was telling the few peeps she has left they must resist. We think it meant to resist the advances of her husband. Anyway, it was weird because her left eye was looking into the camera on her right and the right eye was looking into the camera on her left. Spooky.

In Hawaii a judge has agreed to hear the first challenge to President Trump's new travel ban. But first it had to be explained to the judge what a refugee is since Hawaii doesn't have any. They just have too many liberals.

Rep. Nancy Pelosi (D-Weirdville) is saying she received a text from an interplanetary alien in which the being from another planet (the alien, not Pelosi) has information regarding the Trump-Russian connection.

It was revealed today that Rep. Paul Ryan (R-Turncoat) is, in fact, Toni the Tampon.

Apparently, sometime during the seven minutes of the transfer of the United States presidency from Barack Obama to Donald Trump, the role of president changed. Now anything Trump does that Obama did for eight years, is not okay.

This was a headline today "Legislation introduced by Texas state Rep. Jessica Farrar (D-Loony Bin) would impose a $100 civil penalty for "masturbatory emissions" and "considered an act against an unborn child, and failing to preserve the sanctity of life," the bill reads. Of course the impending fine has caused men all over the state of Texas to whack off before the bill becomes law. People are being told to be careful where they walk so that don't slip and fall.

After the damaging taped revelation in which House Speaker Paul Ryan stated he will not support Trump, it is time for Ryan to go the way of Eric Cantor and John Boehner. And soon!

Breaking News: A video has been obtained purportedly showing Barack Obama in a pair of coveralls, wearing a Make America Great Again hat installing surveillance equipment in Trump tower. This dispels the claim Obama didn't directly have anything to do with the wire tapping controversy.

If Kim Jong-Un doesn't shut up North Korea is going to become a South Korean parking lot.

Chelsea Handler said this:"I wish someone would put Kellyanne Conway in a microwave." This coming from someone who acknowledged her grandfather was a Nazi!

How can any politician talk about Social Security going bankrupt when they all conspired to dump over $5 trillion into the Middle East conflict in the last dozen years?

The problem with the Trump-Ryan relationship is Trump is working for America while Ryan is working for special interests.

Why does CNN have both Chris Cuomo and Sally Kohn? Chris says enough dumb shit so when they bring on Sally it's like piling on.

I get up everyday to check for two things 1) what new awesome thing Trump has done and 2) what silly thing the liberals have done.

I guess Snoop Dogg gets to make videos about assassinating our president as casually as he gets to fling around the "N" word. It is the typical double standard enjoyed by those on the left. Do as we say not as we do. And if you don't do as they say, liberals will crucify in any way they can. Back to the kitchen Dogg.

Why does CNN have both Chris Cuomo and Sally Kohn? Chris says enough dumb shit so when they bring on Sally it's like piling on.

CNN's Jim Acosta crapped in his thong again because he couldn't convince the White House to showcase him on camera at press briefings.

Bill Kristol, head traitor at The Meekly Standard, reminds me of the time I was constipated. For two days I was in terrible pain and when I finally went, out popped this little turd. Bill Kristol is a little turd that pops out and causes a lot of pain.

A new poll out today shows Trump's approval rating is 100% among actual Americans.

Hillary Clinton said she's "coming out of the woods." Is that what they call it these days?

Politically correct Europeans, and I'm sure Americans, are calling Muslims Asians. I wonder how actual Asians feel about that.

I hope artificial intelligence produces idiot proof robots that we can use in place of politicians.

Having the FBI investigate possible interference in an American election by Russia is like me and my man cave regulars getting hammered and trying to determine if Lee Harvey Oswald acted alone in the assassination of President Kennedy.

As the number of accusations and investigations increase, the more we realize how clueless our FBI is and how manipulated they are by our spy agencies. They are looking more like rent-a-cops than law enforcement officials. Embarrassing for America.

Gallup's recent poll showing President Trump has a 37% approval rating was taken among the three staff from Nancy Pelosi's office who happened to be in CNN's break room where the poll was conducted.

It's now official. The world no longer has to put any kind of adverb before the political term "The Left." Since all "The Left" is now extreme any adverbs would be superfluous, just like "The Left" is.

It was just revealed that Rep. Nancy Pelosi has in her office an aquarium filled with red herring.

In front of all of America FBI Director James Comey pulled the "Wouldn't say shit if he had a mouthful" act when being questioned by Congress. We are finding out that the United States is an active member of the Corrupt Nations Club.

Standing together at a podium today was Rep. Nancy Pelosi and Rep. Maxine Waters. Are you still going to tell me you're not concerned?

Every day democrats and republicans alike say stupid shit. So what is the point of confirmation hearings? People who say stupid shit typically ask dumbass questions.

If everyone agrees the actions of a Supreme Court Justice should be non-partisan, why are almost all the questions asked in a confirmation hearing, partisan?

Headline: "Eighty wealthy New Yorkers including George Soros, Steven Rockefeller, and Abigail Disney are asking the state to raise their taxes." There is no law against quietly donating money to the United States Treasury so why would you announce it in the news that you believe taxes should be raised? Just shut up and fork it over.

In Congress the Gang of Eight has expanded and is now referred to as the Gang of Traitorous Assholes.

Headline: "Turkish President Recep Tayyip Erdoğan has warned the European Union (EU) that if the diplomatic spat between Turkey and several European countries continues, Europeans won't be able to walk their own streets safely." Turkey is a NATO member, United Nations member and is currently being considered for European Union membership. Now chew on that for awhile, progressives.

Well, Trump is right again. It's been revealed there was surveillance but they are calling it "incidental collection" as if they were only talking to democrats. The rest of us see right through that lawyer spin bull shit.

Peeping Obama was watching everyone at home and abroad. And it starts with him because he was the boss. He can blame it on everyone but himself but we know better, most of us anyway.

Ya gotta wonder how much stupid you can get inside a big body like New York Mayor Bill de BullShit.

It's contagious. Whatever Rep. Nancy Pelosi and Rep. Maxine Waters suffer from, MSNBC host Chris Wallace now has.

It was reported today that the government will be shutting down due to the constant investigating the democrats and republicans are doing. There is no time left for anything else.

CNN and MSNBC got caught using the same "live" guest at the same time. Duh, they were twins.

CNN "concludes" investigation into a Russian-Trump connection is inconclusive. That is usually what happens when you investigate made up shit. Unless of course you create a made up conclusion which is what fake news outlets usually do.

CNN announced they will be "suggesting" a connection between President Trump and Vice President Pence. Details at 11:00.

MSNBC is reporting they have uncovered tweets by Donald Trump from before Twitter was invented.

When you consider that Trump is up against the republican fifth column led by Paul Ryan, the Obama and Clinton leftovers, the whole of the democrat party and the wealthy donors, it is a wonder he can do what he has done thus far. Without these impediments he could easily be the best president in our history.

The liberals must sit at home with a dictionary putting together all the stupid names they have been coming up with to label conservatives.

Quick fix: The US and its Asian allies should build islands surrounding the ones China is building in the South China Sea.

A woman was arrested for attempting to jump the White House fence for a third time in a matter of weeks. Reporters reveal the woman is Rep. Nancy Pelosi (D-Loony bin).

Former Vice President Joe Biden, never at a loss for words, said he probably could have beat Trump. Yeah, and if my aunt had a dick she would be my uncle.

A study has "found that teens who start smoking marijuana early have impaired cognitive development and even respiratory diseases." That explains democrats.

Why do two political parties still control all politics?

The sun came out today and somehow to those on the Left it has to do with the Right's racist attitude. The fact is breathing is racist to the Left if it is being done by someone on the Right. I think we need to all get closer to a center where we can behave like adults.

Rep. Luis Gutierrez (D-Turdville) was up all night thinking up his latest brain fart. He now claims sanctuary cities are protected by the 4th Amendment. He wouldn't know an Amendment if it bit him in the ass.

Even though all countries bark like junkyard dogs, at the end of the day the big dog is the United States of America.

The non-Muslim world is so stupid and the Muslims know it. Muslims have essentially been casing the world like a burglar cases a house before he breaks in. The sad part is everyone is watching and doing nothing. Saudi Arabia has been financing the building of mosques all over the world. Why?

Missouri Sen. Claire McCaskill, the top Democrat on the Senate Committee on Homeland Security and Governmental Affairs said today we should not ask terrorists trying to get into our country if they are terrorists because they will lie. Folks, this comes from a United States senator. We actually pay these people to come up with this crap.

In what kind of a crazed mind would you accept a 60 year old man marrying a 9 year old girl? This from a religion every liberal is defending. When they are not marrying 9 year old little girls they are throwing gay guys off rooftops or executing their own for blasphemy or honor killing a daughter.

Joe Biden said he is serious about running for president in 2020. He just needs to clear it with the old folks home he will be living in. They have very strict rules.

The mass media claims Putin is standing behind Assad after the Syrian gas attack. How would they know? Assad is 6'2" and Putin is like 5'2" with lifts.

It happened again in Sweden. A crazed man plowed his car into pedestrians and so far five have died. Pictures of the cops leading the dirtbag away looked more like they were walking him to the nearest Starbucks for a free latte on Howard Schultz.

Kim Jong-un took a break from eating and with his 3 chins intact, threatened the United States again. Rumors are that the old farts always following Kim around are actually running the country and they have no idea what they are doing or what the rest of the civilized world is doing. That's why they are dangerous.

Fox Sports Shannon Sharpe, a hero in the sports world for catching a ball, is some kind of god I guess. The way he is shit talking now you would think the guy was the first to separate conjoined twins.

Why is Chicago mayor Rahm Emanuel so concerned about kids graduating from high school? He should be concerned they will live long enough to graduate. Focus, Rahm. Set priorities like stopping the bloodshed in your streets. Start by hiring republicans to help you.

The greatest thing about social media is it is immediate and in your face. And because of that it is more difficult for mass media to control the narrative.

I woke up to find what I thought was a pile of crap from the neighbor's dog on my front lawn. It turned out to be my neighbor's copy of the Washington Post.

Former comedian Bill Maher has been hospitalized for exhaustion after going through the thousands of cases of new Supreme Court Justice Neil Gorsuch in order to proclaim Gorsuch doesn't have any empathy for human beings.

News reports are describing a "shocked Stockholm" after a terrorist attack that killed five. Why would they be shocked? If you willingly open your door to home invaders, what the f*ck do you think is going to happen?

Sometimes political commentator Chris Matthews has taken to wearing a bullet proof vest and has hired security guards out of his fear of Ivanka Trump. His staff should also supply him with a pair of testicles.

After a terrorist car ramming killed 5 in Stockholm the national media in Sweden revealed their Marie Harf terrorism strategy. They said the motive of the terrorist originally from Uzbekistan is currently being examined but did say it could be poverty which dovetails with Harf's conclusion terrorists just need jobs. Between these two brilliant approaches we can rest assured terrorism will soon end.

Also in Sweden this same week a woman was gang raped by four men described as "foreign tourists." That's like calling illegals in California "job hunters." PC bullshit.

Add Little Marco, In the Closet Lindsey with Paul Ryan lurking behind everyone's back with a set of steak knives and you have the makings of the destruction of a political party that is in charge but chooses sabotage instead. WTF?

The new democrat mantra is embrace Muslims and screw the Christians. WTF happened to separation of church and state?

President Trump is hoping to get two full terms giving him eight years to appoint Supreme Court Justices. Since three of them are currently in their eighties (and one can't stay awake) he may appoint at least three more. To assure the Court is conservative for decades to come he is looking for young conservatives in the age group of 15-21 to appoint.

Russia and Iran are warning the United States not to cross any red lines in Syria or else. Right, and Ronda Rousey is going to kick Conor McGregor's ass in the octagon.

Thank you Paul Ryan but we already have a president so you don't need to act like one.

It was revealed this morning that last night there was a slumber party at the DNC headquarters and the featured guest was the Russian Ambassador.

The same people who believed Iran when they said they would comply with Obama's dumbass nuclear agreement (and Iran quickly pocketed $150 billion) are the same people who now believe Assad and Putin when they claim they had nothing to do with a chemical attack. These are people high up in government who buy time shares. Scary.

Don't worry folks, Putin isn't going to do anything to jeopardize his fortune which is said to be the largest in the world.

President Maduro of Venezuela is in Cuba bashing Trump while his people are starving. Cuba's influence on Venezuela goes back to the close relationship of Chavez and Fidel. Now look where Venezuela is. Maduro should be in America bashing Castro. Maybe then Venezuela would get some real humanitarian help rather than socialist advice on how to f*ck your citizens. Well, it's been said (right here, right now) Maduro isn't getting an invite from MENSA anytime soon.

Rep. Nancy Pelosi (D-Loony bin) has said "there is nothing the democrats can work with Trump on." Then what the hell are they going to do? They are getting paid to work. So work.

Rumors are rampant that Seal Team 6 is training to take out Kim Jong-un. Take him out where? To a buffet?

Confused Sen. Liz Warren (D-Faker) wants to know what Trump's ISIS strategy is. How about killing them? Does that work for you?

It was just revealed that the entire eight years that Obama f*cked America, he wasn't wearing a condom. That means the suffering will never end.

Another day goes by and still the only religion killing people is the Muslim religion.

Obama gave us ISIS abroad and MS-13 here at home.

For every donation this month the Democrat National Committee is giving away a pair of rose colored glasses. For larger donations they will throw in a pair of blinders.

The Thugs of Soros have attacked again. This time it was Berkeley but this time the Trump supporters fought back. Hell yeah. The only way to deal with the Thugs of Soros anywhere in the world is to beat the living shit out of them.

Fact: Globalists=cheap labor. Whether they are liberal or conservative, the globalists want cheap labor. They have made their wealth off of the backs of cheap labor, why would they give it up?

America's military brass is debating which weapons to use to take out North Korea's cardboard rockets. My choice would be water balloons. What happens to cardboard when it gets wet? I'm just sayin'.

The dailymail.co.uk reported former president Obama and his wife were out on billionaire David Geffens yacht with Oprah, Tom Hanks and Bruce Springsteen. Officials are still trying to locate anyone who gives a shit. This is news?

MSNBC's Rachel Maddow's newscasts are like a viva voce examination. It doesn't get more boring than that.

At the moment President Erdogan of Turkey succeeded in his country's referendum giving him absolute power, the world heard a big flush as Turkey just went down the toilet.

Europe is now like a living room full of 800 pound gorillas and someone shut and locked the front door. Meanwhile Europeans are trying to get the gorillas to calm down. It's not working.

The halls of the Senate are reeking from the brain farts of John McCain and Lindsey Graham. They seem to be trying to outdo each other in dumbass statements to the press.

I have one thing to say to Sally Kohn. Dude, shut up.

Did you have to kiss your family goodbye today because you were deployed overseas? Did you have to run into a burning building to put out a fire? Were you in a firefight and got wounded while arresting bad guys? Did you have to save someone's life in the operating room after being up for hours working? If these events didn't occur in your life, understand what they mean or shut your f*cking pie hole because people have work to do.

The University of Wisconsin-Madison is now stocking their men's rooms with tampons. On the tampons is a stamp that reads "For liberal men only." Everyone knows that no self-respecting conservative needs one.

There is nothing wrong with Bruce Jenner that a mediocre therapist couldn't cure.

It appears Venezuelan's president Maduro has to have his military explain to him what is going on in the country because Maduro is too f*cking stupid to understand it. Seriously, who destroys a country on purpose? Right, I forgot about Obama.

Former Afghan president Hamid Karzai, made rich by America, has surfaced and is complaining about the America that filled his personal bank account. Take his money and place him back in his hole.

An American University professor who predicted Trump's win now predicts he will be impeached. I also predicted Trump's win and I say he will not only not be impeached, he will win a second term. The real news here is how does this shit get in the news to begin with?

Wow! It turns out not many people outside of Wisconsin actually like Rep. Paul Ryan (R-?). I wonder why?

Authorities have said the FBI is opening investigations into terrorism in all 50 states. Former president Obama asked why not the other 7?

Trump should release his tax returns only after Obama releases his real birth certificate.

Declare cartels a national security risk and tell Mexico we are coming to get them. If Mexico doesn't like it, seal the border. Mexico allows the existence of cartels because of corruption. America must compare the advantages and disadvantages of being the next door neighbor of Mexico.

America's modern history tells us we can't defeat ISIS, Al-qaeda, mobsters, gangsters, sex offenders, rogue nations and California. Maybe Trump will improve this situation if he is given the tools and leeway. Up until now, all others have failed whether they be democrat or republican.

Why is Russia doing fly-bys in Alaska? To scare the Bingo players?

A proposal by a republican congressman to have troops pay a $2400 tax to pay into their GI Bill benefits for school is under consideration. That is the dumbest f*cking thing I have ever heard. The country is giving illegals and refugees a free ride and our warriors get screwed. This is why all politicians are assholes, I don't care what party they come from. I'm a Trump supporter but if he doesn't stop this then he is an asshole. The bombing in Syria, the fighting in Mosul and Raqqa, the actions against North Korea is all American warriors not free riders who don't even have American citizenship. Unf*ckingbelievable.

I would think sportscasters would want to first become believable as experts on sports before they try their hand at something as complex as politics.

Co-Chair of the DNC Keith Ellison did the unthinkable. He criticized Barack Obama. It's bad enough since they are both democrats but even worse because they are both Muslim.

I'm thankful the Boss wasn't the way he is now when I grew up surviving on his music. I might have ended up a democrat.

I have one question for failed quarterback and Champion of Other People's Causes Colin Kaepernick on his tweets, who writes this shit for you?

To the pathetic professor who "laments his sleepless life under Trump" perhaps he should get a dog, maybe a poodle. It could be like a service dog to get him through his emotional ups and downs. Or maybe he should stop being a pussy!

The hypocrisy of liberals rages on in The Huffington Post. Duped last week by the article "Could It Be Time To Deny White Men The Franchise?" it turns out the "feminist activist" who wrote it is a South African man. The HuffPost wasn't going to put up with the embarrassment and tracked the guy down and now he is out of a job. The HuffPost should lend their able investigators to Trump to track down the traitorous Obama leftovers.

Dismissing dictator Kim Jong-un's threats as hyperbole has always, and will continue, to allow Kim additional time to work on the actual nuclear arsenal he is trying to perfect to the point of striking the United States. Are we going to wait until the eleventh hour before doing something?

The mayor of Berkeley, on his seventh visit to the buffet line, stopped long enough to say he supports the shit these freaks in Berkeley are pulling. He is pround to be part of a long tradition of being weird and kinda gross.

Can you imagine Howard Dean and Sen. Elizabeth Warren at a rally together? Ear plugs anyone?

Complaints about daughter Ivanka and her influence in the White House pale in comparison to the fact Valerie Jarrett ran the country for eight years while Obama golfed.

The democrats are calling more witnesses to investigate their claim of a Russian hoax of some sort. So let me count, this would be the fifth dead horse they have beat. Somebody call PETA!

A new poll shows more than half of all Americans have smoked weed. They were described as all democrats except for two republicans.

Rachel Maddow is now the MSNBC resident conspiracy theorist.

Can you imagine Maxine Waters and Al Sharpton sharing a podium at a speaking event?

Military leaders wondered who would take over North Korea if Kim Jong-un is taken out. It would either be Dennis Rodman or Bernie Sanders, a disaster in both cases.

In France, many voters are scared shitless to go to the polls to vote because you may get blown up by a terrorist. Yet many of those voters would vote for a candidate who is partly responsible for the terror threat. That is called a liberal brain fart.

Senator Kamala Harris from California is the new carnival barker in Congress.

Trump has selected a black female with a Ph.D, M.A., is a Navy Admiral and happens to be the Deputy Surgeon General. Amazing. Yet the left is pooping their pants.

A group of leading psychiatrists at a conference declared Trump a mental basket case. This was determined after an interpreter was brought in to interpret all the quacking.

I am a white Californian and our state's "grateful" Mexicans, including the ones who hold political positions and represent me, call me a white supremacist and Nazi. That's harsh, they don't even know me. I hope my Mexican wife doesn't hear that.

Trump obviously doesn't know how to behave as a misogynist because he is putting a lot of women in very high level positions in the White House. I don't think that's what misogynists do. And what about the new black Secretary of HUD and the new black Deputy Surgeon General? That's not what a racist does. Either Trump's confused or liberals are.

Pope Francis has gone too far. He has compared refugee camps to Hitler's concentration camps. The Catholics need to reel him in or dump him. He is not a Pope, he is a politician. I can't see Catholics accepting that comparison especially since a war has been declared on Christian beliefs.

The FBI is encouraging people to call an FBI tip line if they see a democrat out after dark.

America has hacked North Korea's computers so when Fatty Kim launches his rockets using Map Quest he will hit China, Iran and George Soros's house.

With the democrats in complete disarray and the republicans in charge of the White House, Senate and House, imagine what Trump could accomplish if he wasn't interfered with by the traitorous asshole NeverTrumpers. Essentially, with their behavior, the NeverTrumpers are saying f*ck the American citizen.

If Rep. Paul Ryan (R-Turncoat) keeps f*cking Americans we are all going to need a morning after pill.

Democrats bitch if Trump doesn't include them and now they bitch when he includes them. They are turning out to be a bunch of bitches.

Sen. Elizabeth Warren (D-Tribal lands) is "troubled" by Obama's $400,000 payment for a speech. The same group offered her $40.

Advice to fascists: If you don't want to hear what other people with differing opinions say, don't listen. Stay home.

The Antifa thugs getting released from jail are admitting to sore butts.

Barack Obama would talk shit for an entire year as president and get paid $400,000. Now he can talk shit for 90 minutes and get the same amount.

The Clintons are suing Barack Obama for appropriating their Speaker for Hire scam.

Mexico is talking about picking a fight with America over The Wall. Good luck with that. That would be like Barack Obama picking a fight with Mad Dog Mattis.

4/29/17: Thousands of Americans marched today to the acknowledgment they were hoodwinked into the climate change hysteria.

Where are all the conservative billionaires? Trump has provided the ground floor to build a conservative media presence all over America and the world. With the liberal media's self-sabotage there is no better time to give the people what they need. Fox News is soon to be CNN 2.0 so that will leave very little in the way of televised broadcasting of a conservative message. It is a winning strategy proven by Fox News. Just repeat it.

As a conservative I used to read the Washington Post and The New York Times daily so I could be aware of what the enemy is doing. But now, it's just silly. It's a comic strip.

This just out: "Larry Kudlow:Trump Needs to Rally Support for Tax Cuts." Why would we have to rally support for a tax cut? He must mean Trump needs to convince the liberals.

The world should have assassinated Mao, Hitler, Pol Pot, Stalin and Kim II Sung to name just 5. In order to remain "civilized", the world allows millions of innocents to die. And now we have Kim Jong-un. What to do?

I am not going to blame Supreme Court Justice Ruth Bader Ginsburg's nutty political statements on her advanced years. I blame it on the fact she is full of shit.

Obama once said he would not leave the White House and go to Wall Street. He also said you can keep your health care plan, he would close Guantanamo Bay, ISIS is Jayvee, blah blah blah blah blah. Now he gets paid $400,000 by Wall Street for 90 minutes of blah blah blah blah blah.

Bill Clinton told Hillary to chill out and suggested they both go out for some pussy.

Liberal followers believe what they are told. They should vet those who are doing the telling.

Breaking news: Former pro football quarterback Colin Kaepernick has been picked up by a lawn bowling team.

Imagine your garbage man stopping his truck on trash day and commenting on what you put in what can. Just pick up the f*cking trash! This is what happened to ESPN. Just talk about f*cking sports!

Obama called Trump and told him about a problem he was having with one of his new neighbors. He needed to deal with it so he asked Trump if he could borrow his balls for the afternoon.

Conspiracy theories about hand signs are alive and well especially the "okay" sign used by Trump. The other day I was scratching my nuts and was accused of being a liberal.

The despicable, traitorous, back stabbing POS republican nevertrumpers efforts to derail Trump are counterbalanced by democrats stepping on their dicks.

The only climate change I want is to destroy the climate of evil. Maniacs like Kim Jong-un want to destroy our planet with nuclear bombs. That is a more pressing problem than a few degrees change in the temperature.

God put Chris Kyle on earth to save lives, he did it and then God brought him home.

California is hiding the fact it allowed millions of illegals to vote and that is why they refuse to turn over info.

Sen. Lindsey Graham (R-Homo) just said the greatest thing. He said Trump will make State Department cuts "over his dead body." So this means he's going to die? Really, what does that mean? Does he have some kind of disease? Is he challenging Trump to kill him? This is sad, I think. I don't wish him to die, I just want him to shut the f*ck up. Traitor.

The New York Times is so full of shit. A headline today says "Trump's 'Very Friendly' Talk With Duterte Stuns Aides and Critics Alike." America talks to all kinds of crack pot leaders. Obama talked to every asshole he could get a number for beginning with Iran.

President Trump, and I don't know why, allowed three reporters from Reuters into the White House to conduct an interview. That interview has now been overshadowed by the attention paid by liberals to something Trump had given the reporters. It was an electoral college map showing what Trump won versus what Hillary won. Libs went into pantie twist mode trying to understand this. I will explain; after five months since the election the f*cktard liberals still don't accept it. Look at the f*cking map morons.

A woman was caught stealing $93,000 for a Brazilian Butt Lift which leads me to the question "Exactly how high did she have her butt lifted?"

I like the way the democrats are operating. It assures the republicans of winning. At some point even the liberals who are not too far gone, will wake up. When you are playing another team in a competition you don't want them to up their game. You want them to keep playing shitty. The democrats are playing shitty.

President Trump's tweeting is getting honest messages out to us little people before the Washington Machine can cleanse the message as they continue to lie to the American public.

Liberals can justify any ridiculous thing they are accused of. They simply reach around and pull an excuse out of their ass.

A female spokesperson for MoveOn.org, a George Soros funded operation, said on television that Trump's first 100 days has taken womens rights backwards. Now exactly how the f*ck did that happen? Two things things this moron pointed out should be noted 1) "the healthcare bills proposed by the Trump administration take away "essential benefits for women" and 2) "defunding Planned Parenthood." First, no healthcare bill has been passed and second, Planned Parenthood is funded. It is misinformation like this that liberals send out to their semi-illiterate constituents who buy it lock, stock and barrel.

Not only is the Trump Administration finding out there was a lot swept under the carpet, they are finding more carpets. This is going to blow up like the MOAB in Afghanistan.

Megyn Kelly is smart and devious. Her first interview as a new NBC correspondent will be of Kim Kardashian. That assures her of millions of Kardashian's followers. It is a slam dunk rather than a challenge that could blow up in her face and reveal her obvious weakness as a correspondent. It is a ratings interview.

If the democrats keep going to the left they will fall off the earth because it is flat. No really, a democrat told me that the other day.

I watched a video of a rescue in tornado torn Texas and whites, blacks and browns came together to save lives. Don't listen to these fringe groups that would have you believe there is all this hatred. Good people are good people regardless of color.

There are Antifa thugs more patriotic than House Speaker Paul Ryan. Ryan spent too many cuddly nights with Rep. Luis Gutierrez and now he's a little bitch. Ryan makes the Clintons look honest.

In a world of political correctness the only ones allowed to spew the most vile words are the ones who force political correctness on us to begin with, democrats.

The democrat leadership is sending House Speaker Paul "The Weasel" Ryan and his band of NeverTrumpers gift baskets and thank you notes for opposing President Trump more than they do. A note from Chuck "I'm an asshole" Schumer said "Thanks, we couldn't f*ck up the presidency of Donald Trump without you."

Michael Moore said if Trump is willing to sit down with a fat, ugly, one brain cell doofus like Kim Jong-un, he should sit down with him because he is a fat, ugly, one brain cell doofus. Fair is fair.

Comedian for democrats Stephen Colbert used the term cock holster last night. That is a term only used by gay men. Hmm.

Australia has their Apex African Gang, America has MS-13 and Europe has Islamic terrorism. This is what you get for flinging your doors open and letting anyone in. This is self -sabotage. Who does that?

Apple is said to have a quarter of a trillion dollars in reserves yet they will do almost anything untoward to keep their labor costs down. How many other corporations do the same? Remember this when you hear news about H-1B workers.

Always remember and never forget Ronald Reagan's famous quote; "The most terrifying words in the English language are: I'm from the government and I'm here to help."

Illegal immigrant activists are going bonkers today because the mother of one of the leaders of the activists, is being deported. This is the reason why: "Rueda's car allegedly had 33 pounds of cocaine in it, and the couple's apartment had $600,000 cash inside, along with an ounce of crystal methamphetamine." The activists say this is unfair. No matter the reason, those who want open borders don't give a flying f*ck who comes across. It's not about good guys and bad guys to them. It's about looking out for your own regardless if "your own" is a dirtbag.

In the end I disliked Obama to a very high degree but I supported him as the President of the United States.

You know when a man is a pussy. It is when the best he can come up with is vile remarks and names. These are guys who couldn't punch their way out of a wet paper bag. They are not in the military or law enforcement but you will find them in the Democrat Party. All they can do is talk and talk is cheap.

You could have one democrat in both the House and the Senate with the rest being republicans and the republicans would still get beat. Time to dump the republican leaders of both the House and the Senate and order some new testicles for the rest of them. Does the word majority mean anything to these guys?

Regarding the budget House Speaker Paul "The Pussy" Ryan said "I feel good about the wins we got." That's like saying "My best friend is sleeping with my girl friend now but at least I had her until now." The budget is a turd and you can't sugar coat a turd.

God Bless the bikers. They have the balls to stand up to the Antifa bitches funded by Nazi George Soros. Hey Sonny in Arizona, call out the dogs that will scare the shit out of Antifa.

I wonder how long and how many nimrods it took to make up the new #blacklivesmatter chant? Were they like in the studio for days coming up with that catchy tune?

Political scientist Michael Moore wants The Rock to run for political office in 2020. Moore has forgot the political disaster called Arnold Schwarzenegger. It wasn't only Jerry Brown who f*cked up California.

Let me see if I understand this; the ones who caused the problems (democrats) are now telling the republican president how to fix them. Unbelievable.

Trump talked to Putin on the phone Tuesday. He needs to call him back and ask why the Taliban emerged today for a new offensive with Russian weaponry.

Stephen Colbert needs to climb down from his soapbox. He's puffing up his chest like he's some badass. He's just a little f*cking dork with money. It's not like he made that money finding a cure for cancer, he tells jokes for a living.

What are these stress balls I keep hearing about? Is that sub-males squeezing each others nuts in order to calm down?

Turkish presidential aide Ilnur Cevik warned that US troops could be bombed by Turkey if we continue to rely on Kurdish forces to fight ISIS. Did this idiot forget the US and Turkey are both NATO members?

Mika Brzezinski and Joe Scarborough of MSNBC are engaged. That officially makes Joe a democrat because he is a sub-male and his wife-to-be is a rabid democrat. Mika has turned down an offer from the President of the United States to officiate the wedding because it is Trump. She is so politically retarded that she would turn down an offer that has been given to so few people.

Stephen Colbert should know, he was Jon Stewart's c*ck holster.

Those on the left who are saying Trump is unfit to be president may have a point. After all, they would know as they watched as their unfit guy ruled for eight years.

Cher, who is purported to have a net worth north of 300 million dollars is complaining Trump's health care plan won't cover her asthma. That's not true but it is unbelievable should would say that. She should just draw money from her own pocket or are they "too deep?"

While the mass media is still obsessing over Trump's reference of President Jackson and the Civil War, the rest of us are still busy trying to find Obama's additional seven states. Which, by the way, he won in both 2008 and 2012 which, in turn, put him over the top.

Excuse me, I would like a tomato, cheese, pickle and a little humility and a lot of regret on my Russian nothing burger please.

This is so funny and typical of the phony French. A news program sent an interviewer into the street and asked what would be considered middle class people in Paris if they support refugees coming into the country. They all said yes but when the program produces a refugee and asks the people to let him stay with them, they all said no.

If you listen to Hollywood, we are pond scum. It is a wonder we are still the most powerful nation that other nations fear or want to be our friend and people from everywhere want to come to America. Why, if we are so horrible?

Kurt Eichenwald of Newsweek and three time winner of The Shithead of the Year award, has said he wishes "GOP family members lose insurance, get tortured and die." You can see why he swept the Shithead awards three years in a row.

Shithead Kurt Eichenwald has tweeted again stating "as one with a pre-existing condition" to substantiate his ridiculous position. As a pre-existing condition I don't think this shithead's hemorrhoids and herpes rate high on the scale. Yet on the upside it is enough to keep the ladies (or men) at a distance.

It's not so much that Hillary lies it is just that she can't tell the truth.

The FCC is considering fining former comedian Stephen Colbert over his c*ck holster remark. The punishment would be Colbert serving as Bill Clinton's c*ck holster for a week. He would certainly see a lot of action.

After her election loss Hillary blamed everyone and everything including her wandering husband Bill and now makes him wear compression underwear.

As the world spins out of control progressive France elects a guy who will keep it spinning. What happens in France, and a lot of bad things will happen, is on them. You reap what you sow.

Obama's new foundation is intended to make him George Soros 2.0. He saw that Soros was more effective than Alinsky because he was able to channel the dollars. Obama will take the Alinsky socialist mind-set and couple it with the Soros financial approach so that Obama can finally push America into socialism. Why not, since it works so well in places like Venezuela.

Are Snoop Dogg and Martha Stewart dating? Something obviously happened to Martha in prison. She gets down and dirty now.

In North Korea Kim Jong-un's uncles (the ones he hasn't killed) are lining up to volunteer to take him out and I don't mean to lunch.

Take a moment of solace, gaze out your window and think of all the serious problems in other countries. Now, take a moment and pick which problems you would like to come to America. Your decision will tell you what political party to register for. If you don't want any of these problems in America, you are a republican. Everyone else is a democrat or a crackhead.

Why is Chris Pratt apologizing to deaf people for saying "Turn up the volume" if Bill Maher doesn't apologize for an incest remark and Stephen Colbert for his homophobic remark?

Officials from the Democrat Party are still hot on the trail of evidence linking Trump to Russia. They are currently digging up the backyard of a house in Des Moines, Iowa as that is where their clues have led them.

In congressional hearings today fired head of the DOJ Sally Yates admitted she initiated an investigation into former National Security Advisor Michael Flynn after hearing from an unnamed source he may have farted in a crowded room. She felt that would place him at risk for blackmail.

Don't expect the Senate to move fast on the health care bill. One look at Senate leader Mitch McConnell and you can tell he ain't going anywhere fast.

It pains me terribly when I hear about a criminal illegal being released by the police rather than to ICE when a request has been made. As a retired member of the law enforcement family I must say in defense of the line officers, this is management and management in law enforcement, the military and anywhere else is peopled with sycophants climbing a ladder. We have all seen it so you know what I mean. The cop on the street, the warrior in a battle zone in the Middle East are just doing their jobs the best they can within the limitations placed on them by a bunch of assholes at the top.

Archaeologists digging for clues to the beginning of mankind inadvertently stumbled upon the largest swamp ever discovered. This swamp stretches all the way across the nation with its origin in Washington, D.C. . This swamp is specific in nature and after extracting DNA samples from some of its creatures it was determined to be part of the democrat family.

Emmanuel Macron, the new president of France, was observed this morning mowing the lawn of Angela Merkel.

If California legalizes marijuana there will be a 5 year back order on Cheetos which will create a black market for mass produced knock-off Cheetos from China.

The most absurd, most ridiculous, most bizarre thing was said by former Muslim president Barack Obama. He called republicans cowards. The mother of all cowards called someone else a coward. After he said it he ran and hid in a Turkish bath house.

All politicians have always been liars. It's part of their training. But now they are getting so sloppy at it, it has become pathetic to the point they can't even convince a crackhead of their bull shit.

Note to republican elites: We like Trump because, unlike you, he is tough whereas you are little bitches working for the globalists not the voters.

75 year old Martha Stewart, Snoop Dogg's shit on the side, has decided in her golden years to become a juvenile delinquent in her behavior. Maybe it was her time spent in prison or Snoop's got her on the gonga or maybe it's just she's a turd.

President Trump is trying to keep America safe (and by default keep the world safe), honor our veterans, upgrade our military, stop crime, create jobs for Americans, lower taxes, establish a fair health benefit plan, do some good for the inner cities and for this he is some kind of monster according to liberals. So what is Obama since he didn't do any of that?

MSNBC commentator Chris Matthews has caught whatever Nancy Pelosi and Maxine Waters have.

Countries that put their militaries in parades are trying to prove a point. If you are truly a badass you never show your hand.

The Grand Pontificator aka Barry Sotero, is on the road again. He's preaching to anyone who will listen or can stay awake. It is the same bull shit he preached for eight years as America's president. It's nonsense. He likes to talk and now he gets paid even more to talk. The frightening aspect of it is that some people will actually listen.

If the Hollywood elite are so determined to have the arts funded, they should do it themselves. They have money to burn, why lay it on the middle class taxpayer?

Ironically, former FBI Director James Comey is blaming his dismissal on the Russians. His only reponse, "Damn, I missed that one."

The Senate Intelligence Committee is conducting so many hearings on the polluted environment we know as Washington, there is a fear they will run out of intelligence, meaning their own. Some on the committee who started with very little to begin with have already run out.

It was confirmed today that former comedian Stephen Colbert is the child of Jon Stewart. Why Stephen did not inherent his father's comic genes is a question that will probably never be answered.

A national cry went out for "Get a Life" since half the nation (and you know which half) are now protesting the rising of the sun as well as everything else imaginable. The protesters, who are now constantly protesting and only taking breaks to load their crack pipes, are the ones out of work due to Paul Ryan's personal crusade to import foreign workers.

Sen. Chuck Schumer (D-Loonybin) was asked why he insists on wearing those ridiculous glasses. He claims he is transgendering into a grandmother.

There was a mistake in reporting regarding former president Barack Obama's trip to Italy for a $3 million speech about the climate. After disembarking from a private jet and escorted by a 14 car caravan, it was said Obama was protected by 300 police officers. That's corrected to say 300 Jihadists.

Condaleezza Rice appeared on The View the other day and it was obvious the combined IQ scores of the hosts wouldn't even come close to the IQ of Rice.

A drive is underway to collect donated testicles for those republicans who have lost theirs and are not standing up for their republican president. They are being beat up by the likes of Maxine Waters, Nancy Pelosi and crackheads claiming to be anarchists.

As a conservative I support other conservatives unless they cross a certain line. A conservative that is not true to the conservative cause is no different than a Sunday Christian. The #NeverTrumpers in the republican party are Sunday Christians. We need to vote them out or shame them into submission beginning with McCain and Graham.

Once Trump threw his hat into the ring of politics who would have thought it would result in the exposure of Washington as a cesspool. Regardless of party affiliation, we continue to learn American politicians are white collar criminals at most and immoral, unethical bastards in the least. From Hillary and her crew to Ryan and his traitorous #NeverTrumpers, it is a wonder the government functions. I am embarrassed, angry and ashamed of these charlatans.

The engagement of Mika and Joe on MSNBC's Morning Joe is already turning Joe into a beta male. In a couple of more weeks Joe will just sit and nod like a bobble head doll.

In California an Orange County Sheriff's helicopter warned bathers swimming near the coast that there was 15 or more sharks circling near the surf line. Noting the sharks were democrat, all the republicans immediately got out of the water.

If you believe the code stolen from the NSA that is now being used as ransomware was anybody other than a deep state operative at the NSA, then you need to go to rehab and soon.

North Korea fired a ballistic missile today as part of their provocation program. They say it traveled 435 miles when, in fact, it traveled 4.35 miles and took out a labor camp. Oops!

The democrats must think that at some point everyone else is going to suddenly say "Hey, you are really making sense with all this stupid shit you are saying." Why else would they keep doing it?

Note to morons: If you think the problems we have now cropped up over the last four months, you are a moron. These problems developed over the last sixteen years as a result of the poor leadership of George W. Bush-R and Barack Hussein Obama-D. The political elites know this, the mass media know this but apparently you don't. Even if he wanted to, Trump or any other human being could not do all this harm within a few months.

If the United States prosecuted hate the way Europe does, we would run out of politicians.

A ball check was ordered of all the republican men in Congress. The DOJ could not specify a crime they were committing only saying that the manner in which they are behaving is just not right and indicative of men who have lost their way.

It appears the only sane people in America are the Trump supporters who reside in Podunk, USA.

A tweet a day keeps the media away...so the real business of America can get done without media interference.

This week Sen John McCain wrote an op-ed criticizing Secretary of State Rex Tillerson's approach to foreign policy. In doing so McCain revealed his own limited intellect and allowed Tillerson to highlight the depth of his. Talk about shooting yourself in the foot.

Note to Chris Wallace at Fox News: In response to your comment that there is so much chaos at the White House they don't even answer their phone. It's only when you call they don't answer.

Barack Obama spent a good part of eight years traveling the world on the taxpayers dime talking shit about Americans and yet everyone is concerned about Donald Trump tweeting. Grow the f*ck up.

Sen. Lindsey Graham (R-Looneyville) said Trump needs to drop the Russia thing and stop tweeting. Graham needs to borrow a pair of balls from a real man, strap them on and act like a conservative and stand up for his republican president.

American traitor and BFF of Barack Obama, Chelsea Manning, will return to active duty upon release from the shortest sentence ever applied to a traitor. Upon return to active duty Manning's job should be cleaning the latrine, all of them.

After a long winter's slumber that lasted eight years, ICE is doing the job they were hired to do.

When the democrats try to use the flawed argument that Trump is in collusion with Russia and Russia interfered with the 2016 election they conveniently forget America, more than any other nation, has interfered in untold numbers of nations and their business. From nation building to overthrowing governments to assassination attempts, to dropping the bomb, no other country gets in people's business like the United States. The US government is the world's biggest bully and now that globalism is all the rage, we are not going to stop unless someone like Trump stops it. Trump knows we can be a great nation without doing it the wrong way our elected officials have always done it.

Former Director of National Intelligence James Clapper and Obama's favorite butt monkey is on television every day denouncing Trump because he was not told Obama is no longer the president and he is out of a job.

In politics you can use one page or two pages or 500 pages to state your position but it doesn't matter if it is bull shit. Bull shit is bull shit however you describe it. Politicians use eloquent speech to state bull shit. What a waste of eloquent speech.

Why would anyone give a flying f*ck about what an athlete or coach in professional sports has to say about politics?

Jason Chaffetz, rumored to be the older brother of Bret Baier, is said to be taking a job with Fox News (soon to be CNN 2.0). This is a good thing as he is not supporting his president and instead decided to be a turncoat along with the other POS #NeverTrumpers.

I got your back is obviously a term republicans in Congress are not familiar with.

How many Syrians lost their lives because Barack Obama wouldn't enforce the red line he drew? Today it was revealed that Assad may have murdered thousands and cremated them.

President Trump met with Turkey's President Erdogan and Erdogan called Trump a "dear friend". I would advise Trump to remember one name, Virgil "The Turk" Sollozzo.

As a conservative I am shell shocked at the number of congressional republicans who are cowards. These same cowards will send our sons and daughters to war but won't have the back of our republican president. In a way they are worse then the shithead democrats because all the democrats do is spew bat shit crazy nonsense. You can laugh at that. But the republicans they are burying their knives in the back of the president because they are whores for the wealthy donors.

Whether you like Trump or not, you really have to work hard to ignore the positives of his Administration unless you really don't give a shit if America thrives again as a great nation.

The "Comey memo" is about as legitimate as all the prescriptions by quack doctors for opioids that are causing people to drop dead all over America.

Just so you know, the republicans have planned all along to impeach Trump. It is why they demanded he place Pence on the ticket. I like Pence but he knows what is going on so that makes his image suspect. Sad.

While Trump is promoting Make America Great Again, the democrats and republican Trump haters are promoting F*ck America Again.

Another brilliant idea:Let's impeach a president based on a memo from a disgruntled fired employee who practiced politics on the job. Can someone define banana republic for me?

Calfornia's governor Jerry Brown just called the California taxpayer a freeloader because we object to his 12 cent gasoline tax on an already nation high cost for a gallon of fuel. If you have follwed Brown's life, for him to call anyone else a freeloader is funny. The man is the epitome of freeloading.

I am a conservative registered as an independent and I cannot believe what big pussies the elite republicans are. They hate Americans. The democrats are harmless blowhards but the republicans are thugs.

The rumor is false. Thanks to fake news the rumor that Bill Kristol succumbed to brain farting, is false. The revelation of the false rumor brought an early end to parties being thrown all over the United States with the theme of The Wicked Witch Is Dead.

The democrats are making Podunk, USA look like an enclave of the intelligentsia.

Could someone please remind me of Paul Ryan's and Mitch McConnell's accomplishments? For some reason they have slipped my mind. I'm sure there are some, I just can't recall. Maybe a memo from James Comey will help.

A greater chance than impeachment would be Donald Trump quitting and saying "I don't need this shit." He is surely surprised at the mess he inherited as most Americans with a brain cell are.

If President Trump is surrounding himself with traitors it is because someone is advising him. The real culprit in this saga, is the advisor. Shit can that person and ASAP.

The reason why Fox News anchor Kimberly Guilfoyle would be so great as the White House Press Secretary is because she is used to dealing with assholes on a daily basis i.e. Juan Williams and Bob Beckel. Plus, she wouldn't be beholden to Reince Priebus who is beholden to Paul Ryan who is beholden to wealthy donors and Luis Gutierrez.

Let me remind you, when you cringe at the words and behaviors of so many of Washington's politicians and pundits remember, these are grown men and women with college degrees selected to serve the citizens of America.

Milwaukee County Sheriff David Clarke has been selected by President Trump to help lead Homeland Security. I don't know about you but I already feel safer. The Sheriff, by example, will show others how to be loyal. Trump needs more loyalists around him, the Sheriff is a great start.

Rumor mill: The rumor is Obama told friends Trump is a bull shitter. Let me get this right, the mother of all bull shitters is calling Trump a bull shitter. The bull shit is getting deeper.

Maybe establishment republicans and their little followers wouldn't get their panties in a bunch over Trump if they didn't wear panties.

Everyone hold the phone. Don't go off half-cocked with your opinion before you have it approved by a second string quarterback or a basketball coach or a laid off ESPN employee or Maxine Waters.

Be careful. If you see a man approach you in a bro-jumper with a man bun, he is a democrat. Take all necessary precautions.

With Trump enjoying 84% republican approval, republican lawmakers were asked why they were still hesitant to get behind the president and in some cases are trying to sabotage the president. Unfortunately, when approached they ran like hell as assholes often do.

Gov. Moonbeam Brown of California, freeloader extraordinaire, is again asking the federal government for money after flipping them the bird. Brown basically says f*ck you to everyone who doesn't agree with him but then he shoves his hand into your pocket to take more of your money for pet projects, illegal immigrants and Brown's own failures as a governor.

Mike Flynn, ever the warrior, has refused to answer a subpoena so a bunch of pussified men and loony toon women can make fools of themselves at his expense. F*ck em, it's all bogus.

The political infighting among republicans is like the Sunnis and the Shites fighting each other.

While the liberals are shouting daily from roof tops, conservatives are huddled in dark rooms whispering. It is time the conservatives put pressure on all those who are trying to sabotage our president and not because it is Donald Trump but because it is America's president. It's about our country, not about a particular political party.

Although it is certainly getting old I still do get a kick out of those who call President Trump stupid. Think about wherever it is you are sitting in your life and you are calling the new billionaire president of the United States of America, stupid. Grab a mirror dumbass.

Exactly who is running the United States government? Is it the Deep State, George Soros, the mass media? It obviously is not the politicians who are there only to gorge on power and wealth. It is like this event is taking place in Washington and it really has nothing to do with the common man and woman in what a democrat called Podunk, USA. It is like the rest of America is a theater and we are sitting here watching a really shitty B movie.

A democrat and republican got caught with their hands in the same cookie jar and it was on to see who could spin it best. The democrat won by pointing out how it was the fault of the Russians and called for an investigation.

Who is President of Turkey Erdogan that he thinks he can bring his brand of thuggery to America? This guy is f*cking with every country around the globe and republicans and democrats alike are sitting there watching it all take place. This guy just created a dictatorship in Turkey and will become Iran 2.0. And Turkey is a NATO member if you can believe it.

The political establishment is working Trump, softening him up in order to get him to play the game their way. They are self-indulgent in their quest for power and money. Trump has to be the outsider to upset that system. He has to remain tough and be careful who he hires. The traitors are everywhere.

As a Trump supporter I have to call fowl on Tillerson and Kelly pandering to Mexican officials. Even if you were to not have any dopers on the American side, the problems in Mexico are monumental. Mexico was just declared the second most dangerous country, corruption is inbred and the elites make it their mission to maintain what amounts to a caste system. Tillerson and Kelly hold talks as if a modicum of cooperation would solve a multitude of problems. Not. Mexico needs to clean up their country. Cartels are terrorists, blood flows in their streets and poverty is rampant. The government is accused of being cartel supported if not created. No wonder the poor Mexican people want to get out of there.

The problem with Washington today is that an outsider came in and started to disrupt things. Republicans and democrats alike are worried Trump will not only find all the skeletons in the closet but also that the closet has been remodeled numerous times to increase its size. They hired Russian contractors to do the work.

In Michigan the ACLU forced a Sheriff, by threatening a lawsuit, to release criminal illegals rather than hand them over to ICE. At the same time in Texas, Border Patrol agents confiscated $8 million worth of liquid meth coming across the border from Mexico with illegals. This scenario happens daily in America. Connect the dots.

Four senators told head of Homeland Security John Kelly to reject requests for H2-B visas. The senators claim the program is driving down the wages of American workers. Well, that's why the damn thing was set up. It's why employers embrace immigrants, refugees and illegals. They are modern day robber barons. Ask yourself three questions 1) Why are corporations hording so much cash? 2) Why are the valuations of corporations making history? and 3) Why are owners and investors reaping never before heard of profits? We now have 96 million workers out of work or underemployed in America. Reason enough to focus on putting Americans back to work.

Unions were created to protect the American worker yet you never hear from them unless they are pushing a democrat candidate. Democrats engineered the unions takeover of the government employee and the result was municipal unions. Without the government worker on their union membership rolls, the unions disappear and so does what amounts to a political PAC for democrats.

Apparently, the United Nations is not concerned that two of their permanent members, China and Russia, of the Security Council are threatening war. Attempts were made to contact the UN but staff won't pick up the phone unless it is a democrat.

ISIS, North Korea, Iran and all the other bad actors who want to harm America are sitting back observing our lack of attention to what is important and instead see the massive amount of attention paid to stupid, childish squabbles between political parties. They are just waiting for their opening to attack. Nothing like aiding and abetting the enemy.

Democrats are setting up a Go Fund Me page to pay off Joe Biden's mortgage so he can run for president in 2020. Well, run is a bit of a stretch because Uncle Joe will be 78 and I doubt he will even be able to run to the bathroom.

Why is anyone engaging Stephen A. Smith in politics when he doesn't know shit about politics? He's just another sports guy that should be talking about what he is hired for, sports.

Writer Stephen King is out with another political brain fart and a reader suggests he receive the Asshole of the Year award. Are you allowed to win two years in a row?

That conversation Alec Baldwin had with God telling him Trump should be impeached, was really a voice mail message of Alec yelling the most vile things at God. Not that Alec would ever do anything like that to anyone, right?

Liberals are crying fowl because Toby Keith is with Trump in Saudi Arabia and will perform at a men only concert. The liberals, who adore Muslim men as long as they come in the form of a refugee, are having a shit fit. Especially writer Kevin D. Williamson who is tweeting down and dirty shit about Toby. Maybe this tough talking badass Williamson will say this shit to Toby's face? HaHaHaHaHa.

A photo of Senator Tom Cotton standing near Senator Ben Sasse gave millions hope that Cotton's remarkable characteristics of a real man would pass to Sasse. Stay tuned but don't get your hopes up because Sasse needs a 100% transformation.

CNN's Chris Cuomo wants "proof" of no Trump-Russia collusion. If anyone watches Cuomo you know he is as dumb as a bag of hammers. He wouldn't know proof if it bit him in the butt. Thankfully, we never have to worry about this Cuomo running for office.

"A U.S. official read notes taken of the conversation to The Times' reporters. Another government official confirmed Trump's general comments." If you see this among the wording of an article you can be sure the premise of the article is total bull shit. Who is the US official, the person who took the notes, the Times reporter, another government official? Who buys this?

Anonymous sources (of course) are now saying they have actually seen the "memo" former FBI Director James Comey wrote to himself about Trump. They found it on the ground outside of a pizzeria in Brooklyn.

If Trump really did call former FBI Director James Comey a nut job, that is a lot more kind than all the vile names Trump has been called. I would rather be called a nut job than a c*ck holster.

After watching numerous interviews of students on college campuses I now believe they are not bastions of higher learning but are actually moron incubators.

Think about this for a moment and this is coming from me, a conservative. If the establishment republicans who were, and are, against Trump have been putting together a coup, and I am convinced they are, it makes the democrats look like harmless babbling idiots. The real threat to our republic are these rogue, and not so rogue, republicans who are dead set against Trump being our president. We have a very serious problem here that good republicans need to wake up to. If these POS republicans are willing to go as far as disrupting our government, it is anybody's guess what else they have done or are willing to do. I think Trump's very presence has opened up a huge can of worms.

Liberals are squawking about an unverified account of Trump calling Comey a nut job. Obama spent eight years going all over the world calling Americans names and liberals never said a damn thing.

Note to possible immigrants coming to America: You might want to think again since the immigrants already here are saying America is f*cked up.

In light of what is going on presently with the attempt to sabotage the Trump Administration it seems silly that democrats were so obsessively concerned people would defame the Obama Administration because he is black.

When losers like Jeb Bush, and others, tell Trump to stop tweeting he is really saying he wants Trump to stop talking to the voters directly. Tweets give the voters immediate notice of what is happening. He by-passes a mass media that would turn his words into fake news and other politicians who would "sanitize" what Trump says to fit their narrative. Tweeting by Trump is engaging the world in real time and it removes the cover of darkness so to speak that the unscrupulous politicians use to conceal their suspect activities.

It is no longer possible for Sweden to celebrate anything publicly without there being a rape or a sexual assault. They brought this on themselves.

Chris Cuomo is at it again. He is in a race with Nancy Pelosi and Maxine Waters to say the dumbest thing possible this week. His "there is no proof of no evidence of Trump-Russia collusion" theory this week is right up there with "you have to pass the bill to find out what is in it" theory. Chris is already shilling for his brother who hinted he may run in 2020. Other than that the guy is just f*cking brilliant!

Anderson Cooper told Jeffrey Lord, a Trump supporting commentator, that Lord would defend Trump if Trump took a dump on his desk. This, coming from a guy that can't take a dump until he removes his butt plug. Seriously, it has devolved into this kind of behavior.

In a gun controlled America the revelation that the United States government is the largest and most prolific arms dealer worldwide, is completely ignored.

Anthony Weiner, who lets his wiener do his thinking, has finally been dealt with. After expending all his political currency it turns out Weiner is just another sick pervert who will go to jail. The fallout from this should prove to be shocking. Believe me, the guy ain't going to jail and not say anything about the people he trusted to keep him out.

Rep. Al Green went to the House floor and requested impeachment of Trump. He looked like he was in the middle of preparation for a colonoscopy.

With the arrest of a high number of bad actors all over America including criminal illegals and gang bangers, it is obvious Obama put law enforcement into a forced hibernation. Just wait until Trump starts arresting crooked politicians.

If you want to get rid of the leakers in the White House, bring in the Bikers For Trump. All the bikers have to do is round up all the guys with man buns wearing rompers. Those are your leakers. They won't fight back.

Former FBI Director and man child James Comey is now convinced Trump wanted to influence him. It was something about the twinkle in Trump's eye.

Things keep getting worse for Anthony Weiner who has to register as a sex offender, he's already a registered democrat.

The only memo former FBI Director and showboat James Comey will be able to produce is one from his wife telling him to pick up a loaf of bread and a carton of milk on the way home. But to be sure the mass media will somehow involve Russia in that memo.

It was discovered that the unnamed White House Official who was leaking negative information to the press was none other than a janitor in the West Wing who is a registered democrat.

Over the last 16 years the republicans and democrats did such a horrible job in dealing with the war on terror they should not be allowed to interfere while Trump fixes it.

Just so I understand this correctly, Obama goes overseas, trashes Americans and gives money to the leaders of nations he visits. Trump, on the other hand, visits a nation and cuts deals bringing money into American coffers. Hmm.

Trump is destroying ISIS, creating jobs, cutting the fat from government, I can understand why the democrats might be upset.

Nancy Pelosi was overheard talking about Trump in the Middle East. An anonymous source claimed she said "What the f*ck is wrong with these Muslims? They are suppose to hate Trump over the travel ban. Someone get me a sedative."

The US Embassy in Belgium is providing $200,000 through a grant to "promote positive narratives about refugees" in Europe. The grant hopes to "reduce violent extremism and terrorism by promoting a comprehensive approach to address violent extremist challenges in Europe." That is what is referred to as horse shit. Put that $200,000 in a jobs training program in Detroit.

Retired CBS News personality Bob Schieffer grabbed his teeth from a glass and ventured out on the patio of the old folks home and said Trump actually sounded "presidential" in Saudi Arabia. Well, that is tons better than Obama who always sounded presidential but never acted that way.

Another terrorist attack in the UK. Remember when the Muslim mayor of London told the world terrorism is part and parcel of everyday life? Well, the UK participates with other European nations in Refugee Roulette. Since every terrorist attack is committed by a Muslim, you don't know if the next refugee entering the country is a true refugee or an Islamic Extremist.

Every time ISIS commits a terrorist attack, progressives run to coddle "peaceful" Muslims against Islamphobia. And in that coddling is some kind of benefit to the Muslim. So in other words, the "peaceful" Muslim benefits from the atrocity and that is why they don't speak out.

We had eight years of Bush and his leanings towards the left and then we had eight years of Obama socialism. Look where we are. Are you really okay with that?

I don't understand it. Europe lets the refugees in, bad shit happens, Europe lets more refugees in. I may not be brilliant but I know stupid when I see it and Europe is stupid. Stupid kills.

Apparently, and I'm not sure this would do it, wealthy people living in bubbles won't change their position of "we are all one big happy family" until a terrorist bursts their bubble. Honestly, I don't think they give a flying f*ck how many of us commoners die.

When nut jobs like Hillary Clinton and Bill DeBlasio say something like "children will die" as a result of Trump's budget the only people buying that are crackheads and even they are starting to doubt.

Pope Francis should be grateful for Trump because either by default or intentionally, Trump is going to boost the fortunes of the Christian world.

5/24/2017: Mark my words, I think the most dangerous man in the world right now is President Erdogan of Turkey. He is a scammer, bully, dictator and has access to nuclear weapons.

Sen. Mitch "Grandpa" McConnell said he loves Trump's agenda but hates his tweeting. McConnell and Ryan would never tweet because that would allow us to know what they are up to. They prefer the shadows like criminals.

Sen. Elizabeth Warren (D-Loony Bin) just threatened Trump with "You ain't seen nasty yet." What does that mean? Is she going to show up somewhere in a bra and panties? That would be gross.

It would be comical if it wasn't so pathetic. When I read any daily headline of the Washington Post website my mind goes to a room full of reporters brain storming, or rather ass storming, what they can pull out of their asses to report today about President Trump. Seriously, their hatred could not be more obvious. This is not a news outlet, it is the diary of a bunch of progressives made public each day.

If an organization, like CNN for example, is going down the toilet for saying stupid shit it doesn't make sense to double down on saying stupid shit. There is no word yet from new CNN spokespuppet Elmo.

I was just informed, but it hasn't been confirmed yet, we do have republicans in Congress. Their whereabouts at this time is still being determined.

Today in Egypt to celebrate the first day of Ramadan, 35 Coptic Christians were murdered. It won't be mentioned in the mass media unless by mistake. It won't have a fraction of the coverage the 20 deaths at the Ariana Grande concert had. Liberals will largely ignore it except for Christian liberals (what few are left). This is another attack in the effort of Muslims to eliminate Christians. I am no Christian but I know this is bull shit. You morons who don't know history should read a f*cking book.

Canadian Prime Minister Justin Trudeau, Obama's brother from another mother, danced around questions of why Canada is the worst paying member of NATO. It is because Trudeau is following in the footsteps of his hero Obama and funneling Canadian dollars to all the refugees he is inviting into his country.

Nobody has the right to stop an investigation of the Seth Rich murder. As long as the murderers are still on the loose every American is in danger. The democrats, George Soros, mass media, Murdoch sons, corporations have no f*cking right to obstruct this investigation. An investigation is going to conclude it was a political hit.

Sometimes Fox News commentator Charles Krauthammer is full of kraut. His rant about Trump's NATO speech didn't even rise to the level of a Charlie Sheen rant.

Failed presidential candidate Hillary Clinton lashed out with this yesterday regarding the Manchester terror attack "Outraged & angry about this cowardly terror attack on a crowd of young people." Based on her history, she wouldn't know a cowardly terror attack if one bit her in the butt.

A fat little f*cking piece of North Korean shit murdered a 20 year old American kid over a stupid prank. We need to take this asshole out and I don't mean out to lunch.

A sitting member of Congress, Rep. Luis Gutierrez (D-IL), was pictured smiling proudly with Obama released FALN terrorist Oscar Lopez Rivera. Gutierrez should, in the least, be censored for that action. Gutierrez makes Pelosi and Waters look intelligent.

With Fox News moving quickly to the left there will be no main stream media for conservatives. We will have to rely on the internet. With all the bull shit coming from the main stream media, it is helpful to get the straight scoop from Trump tweets. He is our direct connection. Take that away and politicians of all stripes get their cover back to hide from the people.

Just to give you an idea of what Trump has to deal with I will mention a few names. Merkel, Macron and Trudeau. And American liberals were concerned Trump wasn't qualified to be the president. Trump is dealing with these people thinking "these are my peers?"

In an extensive search I found no instance in which a wealthy globalist lost their life to terrorism committed since 9/11. All the people who have died are the ones the wealthy globalists are telling how to live. There has been no terrorist attacks in Beverly Hills or the Hamptons.

You notice how some people just won't go away. They are not asked to stick around but do anyway.

Rep. Paul Ryan has developed a new line of panties for men who have no balls like himself. He is staffing his company with H1-B workers due to the fact he hates American workers.

The former Vice President of the United States Joe Biden openly wished he could take Trump "behind the gym." Knowing the Vice President's groping history speculation is skyrocketing.

Democrats are saying incredibly stupid shit to keep their base, stupid people, engaged. The problem with stupid people is although there is an endless supply, you can't always count on them to show up at the ballot box (see Trump wins presidency).

If you really want to know what white privilege is it is a criminal "gang" made up of elite politicians from all parties and certain wealthy individuals. The thugs are primarily white males with a few exceptions. Their thirst for wealth and power is insatiable. They lack moral fiber and ethical behavior is what they expect others to practice. They are the reason conspiracy theories exist and why many are probably true. Whatever you think in your wildest imagination, could likely be so. This group has particular names attached to them so it is not as if their existence is a secret. The organization is worldwide and nothing happens unless they allow it. They are the most powerful force on earth. That is the real white privilege.

Some facts about North Korea: The Chinese are helping them bigly, it is not Kim running the show it is the old farts, much of North Korea's income is illegal, Kim is hugely wealthy with money stashed all over the world, Kim loves a buffet and has a little dick.

The Hillary thing is getting kind of weird. She lost. She needs to move on. She is embarrassing herself and looking more pathetic each day as a weakling. A president needs to be tough (see Trump and not weak (see Obama). Her own base, truth be known, doesn't want her to run for anything. She needs to ride off into the sunset.

North Korea attempted to launch a ballistic missile but it failed. They now know you can't launch one of these things off the back of a rickshaw.

Recent events at institutes of higher learning such as Harvard or Yale have shown the world that the presumption these people are the best and the brightest is total bull shit. The only thing these guys are good at is making tons of money while f*cking everything up for regular people. That would be you and me.

Trump speaks for millions and millions of his supporters who don't have a soapbox in Podunk, USA. He says what we would like to say.

It was just revealed Notebooks-R-Us was asked to send crates of small notebooks and pens for North Korean Dictator Kim Jong-un's generals. They offered to trade coal for the notebooks and pens since North Korea has no money. They also have no food or common sense.

I asked United Airlines if they would pay me $10,000 to book a flight on their airline and then bump myself. No word yet.

A black Antifa thug shouted down the cops arresting him calling them honkies. That's pretty old school, aren't we crackers these days?

Whenever a serious problem arises in the world the smart guys look at it and say; Let's do this to alleviate this problem but wait...if we do that then over here, where we are making a bunch of money, things will go haywire so scrap that idea. This is the conversation that gets played over and over again and that is why we don't solve problems, we create even more.

Rumor is that all Kim Jong-un needs is an enema. He has been constipated the last three years and it has turned him in to a veritable asshole. The porker cannot stop eating even after he has taken all the food from his citizens.

May Day, a day to celebrate labor all over the world. It should be renamed Asshole Day because that's what everyone acts like on this day.

The United States Agency for International Development (USAID) for years right under Obama's nose (he probably knew) has funded the growing of opium in Afghanistan. The country is the top producer of opium which is used to make heroin. This makes us a de facto drug dealer.

A young man tried a home invasion of a woman 52 years old and 4'11" but it failed miserably. She beat the crap out of him with a baseball bat. His chance of ever getting a man card is now zero.

Not only is Venezuelan President Nicolas Maduro stupid, he looks stupid. He's always got that "What way did he go George" look on his face. He hiked the minimum wage by 60%. There are no jobs or food or anything else for that matter. Every night at bed time an aide reads to him from How To Ruin A Country for Dummies.

I live in California so if Trump raises the federal tax on gasoline and I have to pay that along with Calif. Gov. Brown's already approved tax on gasoline in California, my gas bill will exceed my mortgage.

With technology being what it is in the future a World War will last about 3 minutes if anyone is left to record it.

You know we are failing when it comes to the war on terror when ISIS operates a dating website for its members.

I started to speak and was attacked with complaints from social justice warriors who assumed I was going to say something politically incorrect. After they were finished they said I could go ahead and say what I wanted to say but in the way they say I should say it. I said too late I already farted.

Doctors are now saying talking to yourself is not mental illness. Well, doesn't it come down to what you say to yourself?

We may be close to a cure for one particular type of cancer. The Kardashians television ratings are biting the dust.

After all the talk of diversity, can't we all just get along and we are all one human race, I'm sorry to say we are going in the other direction. Oops!

California prepares to tax space travel and who better to do that than Gov. Jerry "Moonbean" Brown. Next on the table is a proposal to tax the thoughts of Californians. That would be a tax worth paying only because Gov. Brown would know what we think of him.

It's raining in Southern California today. I don't know why but I know it must be the Russians.

You really have to wonder just how braindead people are who commit terrible acts when they know they are on camera.

Dailymail.co.uk headline: "No diapers? No problem! Meet the parents who toilet train their babies from BIRTH by holding them over sinks, toilets, miniature potties and even the side of the road." So 15 years from now it won't be unusual to drive down the road and see grown men and women crapping on the side of the road. Just great. I guess the world is becoming a toilet anyway.

United Airlines was forced to apologize again although I'm not sure why. They mistakenly sent a passenger to San Francisco instead of the correct destination of France. So, what's the difference?

Just in: Michael Moore was tackled by local police outside a GOP meeting in which he hijacked a dozen chocolate eclairs meant for participants at break time.

I'm thinking maybe two more no-go zones in Sweden and there will be no Sweden. They are self-destructing. And the migrants are laughing all the way to Mecca.

Farmers in rabidly progressive California are complaining that their intentional business model that relies on immigrant labor aka cheap labor is being impacted by Trump's approach to the immigration problem. These guys are a major component of our illegal immigration problem. They are right up their with the dopers. The farmers who have been around for awhile have had an opportunity to change either their business or business model, the newer guys came in knowing they were going to use illegals. Do I feel for them, no. Millions and millions of Americans, many of them in business, have survived without immigrants legal or otherwise.

The CBS interview between John Dickerson and General James Mattis was a classic interview between a beta and alpha male. You could tell, one wrong thing from Dickerson and Mattis would rip off his head and shit down his neck. Semper Fi.

This just in: Secretary of State Rex Tillerson aka T-Rex, accidentally (we think) ran over the foot of former Secretary of State John Kerry, with his Harley during the Rolling Thunder ride. Mr. Kerry was on his way to a meeting, on a Vespa, of feminists who are part of The Resistance.

The mass media are going crazy today because they haven't seen a tweet from Trump. They don't know what to do.

If you don't think the mass media is only about identity politics, why would the Murdoch sons take the top ranked (by far) news channel and let it collapse to third place only to rebuild it to resemble all the others unless you care more about your political opinion than your business model? And it is not like they are going to bring anything new to the discussion.

MSNBC's pseudo republican Joe Scarborough was said to be barking like a dog this morning until Mika looked down in her lap and shushed him.

Scientists are currently working on a project that would use stem cells from a republican to regrow a backbone in a democrat.

Good "peaceful" Muslims who insist the world should not chastise them for what Muslim terrorists do are not stepping up to condemn or distancing themselves from the terror. They are sitting quietly and refusing to take any action or accept any blame. We saw this with the Catholic church and their non-action with perverted priests.

In Europe progressives have decided to fight terror with "teddy bears and candles." I don't know if they were stuffing grenades into the teddy bears and planned to set terrorist hideouts on fire with the candles. If they actually mean to fight terror with love, good luck with that. These terrorists ain't looking for love. They plan to kill us.

Manlet Macron, newly elected leader of France, thinks he is Mini-Trump. In office two weeks and he's acting like a badass around world leaders. Who's coaching this little shit? His mom...I mean his wife? Has he forgot he is the leader of France? He ain't the leader of America or Russia.

Why are progressives applauding Merkel? Because she talked shit to Trump? Germany is a f*ck up waiting to happen. Just look at their history of shooting themselves in the foot. And now Merkel is ruining Germany. She is like a spoiled child that wants everything for nothing. She wants the protection of the EU and the US. And why is Merkel speaking for Europe?

I will be the first to say we must have a diversity of political opinion to survive as a true democracy. But at some point there has to be a certain restraint to our comments. A line is crossed when we advocate violence vocally or through innuendo. This orchestrated resistance to the election of Donald Trump is not American.

Sen. John McTurd (R-AZ) is doing his best impression of Obama as he travels the world and belittles our president. There should be a rule that sitting politicians can be censored when they do that.

Today Hillary is blaming the debacle in Venezuela for losing the election. Even Bubba doesn't understand this one.

Rep. Al Green from Texas was asked recently why he always looks like he just got the worst news of his life. He said in all those pictures he is actually smiling. He said this look comes from Botox treatments.

The website dailymail.co.uk keeps us informed of how many and what women Scott Disick is banging and yet feel qualified to comment politically on President Trump.

What really sucks is how much richer the rich liberal assholes will become once Trump does his magic. It started the day he won. While these dickheads are putting Trump generated dollars in their banks they trash him.

The regret may be too much to handle. If the republicans would have done to Obama what the democrats are doing to Trump, maybe we would have had only four years of devastation instead of eight. True, it would have required the republicans to debase themselves and quit their jobs in order to have the time and that is not in their DNA.

Those pesky peaceful Muslims are at it again killing 90 of their own in Afghanistan today. More than a billion Muslims in the world and they are allowing thousands of terrorists to wreak havoc in the name of Islam.

Little shit dictator Kim Jong-un waves like he wants to say "Hi there fellas."

The loonies on the left are freaking out over what they say is a terrible misspelling by President Trump on Twitter last night. Morons, if it is a made up word, how would you know if it is misspelled? Get a life.

Imagine a woman buried in the earth up to her waist surrounded by 30-40 men who are about to stone her to death despite her being a victim of rape. This is Pakistan 5/31/2017. These are the "peaceful" Muslims glorified by liberals.

The reason officials in El Salvador are in a panic with all the returning gang members is because they were convinced they dumped them on America forever.

Who needs terrorism when you have Chicago? This weekend Chicago turned into a shooting gallery for armed thugs and a shooting gallery for thugs to shoot drugs in their arms. Make America Great Again with the exception of Rahm Emanuel's Chicago.

Failed candidate Hillary Clinton said today her email investigation was a nothing burger. This is her arrogance showing because she believes her political class will always protect her. This is why we have to get her in a court room and let the chips fall where they may.

Even if President Trump does something good the media attacks him as if he has an ulterior motive.

It's so funny because right after Rep. Nancy Pelosi (D-Loony Bin) said it was "hard to call Donald Trump President," millions of people said it was hard to call Pelosi sane.

Even the most progressive politician in Europe knows they would rather have America as a friend than a foe. So frumpy little Merkel and manlet Macron can carnival bark all they want because in the end America is the biggest, baddest, most awesome nation on the planet so you want to be our friend.

The list of who to blame for Hillary's loss is now so long she has decided to turn it into a book similar to War and Peace.

Does Sen. John McTurd of Arizona do any actual work or does he just travel the world on the taxpayer dime to trash Trump? It's kind of like Barack Obama trashing Americans.

Hillary Clinton woke up this morning and added the Avon ladies to her list of people to blame for her loss. She claims the group has always leaned right.

Democrat operatives are saying Hillary will run again in 2020. Unfortunately, her health will not permit this. Doctors have discovered she suffers from myshitdon'tstinkitis and the voters are aware of this and that is why she lost the first time.

Regarding the Paris Climate Agreement the businesses that are against Trump pulling out are globalists. They make their money operating globally. One of them is Elon Musk, who has probably hoodwinked his way into billionaire status. His company makes worldwide sales. None of these companies has gone on record regarding if and why they support the climate change mafia. The Paris Climate Agreement is mostly about making lots of money for the already wealthy. Al Gore is a perfect example of someone who has used suspect climate change assertions to create personal wealth. The person on the street has not a clue about what is in the agreement. This has always been a political/business issue about money.

What former Jeopardy champion and children's book author Ken Jennings should worry about after his dumbass remark to 11 year old Barron Trump is if Barron will beat the shit out of him. Have you seen the guy? He also models rompers. God forbid he ever gets stuck in a wet paper bag.

Tyler Shields, the douche bag that took the gruesome photo of old hag Kathy Griffin holding Trump's head, says he can't censor himself. You know, it's the old artsy, fartsy excuse that artists use. We have to censor ourselves but they don't have to because they are "special" like a f*cking hemorrhoid.

I was already a fan of Kevin Hart the comedian but now I am a fan of Kevin Hart the man. No matter what political party he belongs to it is what he said in an interview that won me over. He said he doesn't comment on politics because he would alienate a portion of his audience. Well said. He has a ton of conservative fans but he refuses to do what other celebrities do and that is to be so insistent on getting their political views publicized, they ignore the feelings of their conservative audience. The conservatives that helped propel them to success. It's like George Lopez dumping his wife after she gave him a kidney so he could stay alive. Thanks for the respect Kevin, I wish you even more success.

If you notice, all the people freaking out about Trump dumping the Paris Climate Agreement are on the other side of the political spectrum. These people freak out when Trump wakes up in the morning.

The three musketeers of Macron, Merkel and Gentiloni of Italy said after Trump backed out of the Paris Climate Agreement that there would be no re-negotiating. Watch the clock it is just a matter of time.

Joe Biden is considering a run in 2020. His line-up of sponsors is impressive beginning with Depends, Geritol, Medical Alert Systems, Meals On Wheels, Canes-R-Us, Miracle-Ear Hearing Aids.

The people who are furious over Trump's decision on the Paris Climate Agreement are the same people that want you to hug a refugee today, want open borders, say whites are privileged, forbid you to say certain words, want to pay salaries to terrorists, claim conservatives are racist, misogynist and bigoted, want guys to go to the bathroom next to your daughter, etc.

Author and humorist David Sedaris is utilizing the Kathy Griffin Method of How To Promote Yourself. He has said he hates Trump and wished he had killed him. Kathy is a comedian and Sedaris is a humorist. Maybe they should let humor guide their life rather than hatred.

To kick off her new show Megyn Kelly wrangled an interview with America's favorite thug, Vladimir Putin. She went full on blonde bimbo for the debut.

Kathy Griffin, probably on the advice of attorney Lisa Bloom, is playing Hillary Clinton. Her new found troubles are the fault of the Trumps and white, racist, sexist men. It's like listening to a tape of Hillary.

I am not sure who high profile democrats (and that includes Arnold) are trying to connect with by sounding like 13 year old teenage boys who just discovered swearing. Do they feel this is the only why they will be taken seriously?

To all the religious left who object to Trump's dumping of the Paris Climate Rip Off, I will have you remember it is God's Plan. This is the way religion deflects criticism so it should apply here.

Arnold Schwarzenegger is calling for a "grassroots revolution" after the US departure from the Paris Climate Scam. But first, he has to finish "interviewing" new housekeepers.

Rep. Nancy Pelosi (D-Confused) is a POS because she insists on using Trump's grandchildren to make a political point. Leave the children out of your vile political discourse.

Kathy Griffin is just being a democrat when she blames the victim. Everyone knows when a democrat is caught with their hand in the cookie jar, it is the cookies fault. Ask Hillary.

Hillary Clinton talks about flying planes like she's grabbing a bicycle to peddle down the street to the local market. Now that is being concerned about the environment.

U.S. Rep. Trey Gowdy has been named to the House Permanent Select Committee on Intelligence. He's like a Trump Mini-Me. He speaks the truth and does it brutally versus cowardly liberals who are into name calling but won't back up their shit.

This just in: California Gov. Jerry Brown's brain has taken a turn for the worse. After suffering from recurring brain farts for well over 3 years the Governor is finally at the point his brain is just not working. From all the changes he is proposing he will have to find a way to declare California its own country.

A roomful of prominent democrats were meeting to determine their next step in the process of getting anyone to believe in their Russian collusion theory. In desperation, they all dropped their drawers and started pulling theories out of their butts. This is how pathetic it has become.

If the European Union chief shit talker Jean-Claude Juncker, who moonlights as a f*cking moron, wants the Paris Climate Scam so badly there are still 199 countries left in the deal. America is only one country. Why do they care? Because they were going to make America their financial butt monkey.

The real reason Trump pulled out of the Paris Climate Accord is because it is one of the biggest brain farts from the democrats in years. The deal didn't do shit but put American dollars in foreign pockets and when that happens the globalists profit. It's a formula.

It was rumored today that little shit dictator Kim Jong-un overdosed on chocolate eclairs.

If we are not going to prosecute them then we must at least out them. I am speaking of the US, foreign countries, multi-national corporations and wealthy individuals funding terrorism. The way the US funds terrorism is by supplying armaments that always seem to end up in the hands of terrorists. We also do it by not tracking the millions of tax dollars going into Afghanistan and Iraq and when we purchase oil from a nation we know is feeding dollars under the table to terrorists.

Nebraska RINO Ben Sasse (R-Traitor) wasn't cringing as he claims when former comedian Bill Maher called himself a "house n*gga." Sasse was laughing with the audience. Liar.

At some point, and many of us feel we are there now, the half empty, half full glass becomes completely empty. That is when we no longer can say Islamist extremism but instead must say the truth which is routine Islamist terrorism because it has become "part and parcel of life in a big city."

While the world has serious problems for the average Joe, the democrats and their globalist enablers continue to focus on their own attempts at personal gains to fullfil their vision. It is simply too bad the rest of us get caught in the crossfire.

There are whispers in Washington that the leaker is Paul "The Weasal" Ryan. There has been no denial.

We are spending valuable energy and resources on made up shit rather than focusing on the real problems. This is a diversion designed to cripple the current Administration's efforts to deal with those real problems. You can either be concerned about the political leadership of your chosen party, which is encamped in a city that might as well be another planet, or you can be concerned about your children and the future. Choose what is important to you first and then see how the different political parties address that.

If only John McCain and Lindsey Graham along with their #nevertrump troops were as courageous as Nikki Haley. We can always dream.

Billionaire Michael Bloomberg should put the $15 million he pledged to climate control into a jobs training program (run by conservatives) in the inner city. That climate is in need immediately. If he is joined by all the billionaires who are throwing away their money by donating to losing or fictitious causes, we can do substantial work in our inner cities in America. Tell a struggling minority about your concern for the environment and he will stare at you with a blank look because he or she is hungry and not concerned about an iceberg.

If something actually got done in Washington how would we know if the media won't report it?

The one thing you can't deny about Vladimir Putin is he cuts to the chase. He has no desire to engage in silliness and use politispeak to make his point. He calls it the way he sees it. Bull shit is not hard to identify.

Out of all the constant, hateful speech that Bill Maher spews it is only when he uses the "N" word that people speak out. That is the rankest form of discrimination we can practice. To selectively enforce hateful speech is hate itself. We cannot allow one particular group to corner the market on victimization.

It was reported "a fact" broke into the CNN press room but was immediately arrested and removed.

President Trump has massive battles on four fronts 1) democrats 2) mass media 3) nevertrump republicans and 4) globalists. We can get into how each one of these causes him problems but we see it unfolding in real time each day. The world is fully aware of it and allows it to continue. What it says about Trump is he is effective despite this which will have his legacy make Obama's look silly.

Chief Justice John Roberts just said the Justices don't work as republicans and democrats. What he is really saying is Americans are so stupid they would believe something as absurd as what he just said.

It is obvious now that Trump's Middle East trip was the vehicle to tell the Middle Eastern powers he knows what the f*ck they are doing and it better stop now because there is a new (and real) sheriff in town. This is revealed by the reception he received and the fact six of the major powers just cut off Qatar for funding terrorism. It has always been suspected they did but Obama let it slide. Trump said no way. Let the testosterone flow.

As long as we provide the safe haven of victimhood to "peaceful" Muslims they will not help us in the war on terror committed by other Muslims. If they are scared straight they will fall into line.

Every month that passes we experience more threats and actual terror attacks. We, meaning the western world, are having to upgrade our defenses and add a new type of defense for a particular threat. With your calculator in hand add two plus two and see that it adds up to the Muslim refugee crisis. It's a no-f*cking-brainer.

Every time a European lights a candle or places a bouquet of flowers or a teddy bear at a makeshift memorial, they admit defeat in the eyes of a terrorist. You must say nothing, do nothing and then in the dark of night, take revenge. This is all they understand and is what has defeated them over the course of 1400 years.

Today Dr. Gorka, a spokesperson for the White House, had to school CNN Host Chris Cuomo about Trump's travel ban. Last week a fifth grader had to school Cuomo on life itself.

The fact the democrats can effectively hold up the business of Congress shows just how pathetically wimpy Paul Ryan and Mitch McConnell are. What is the point of securing the majority in the Congress and also have the White House if republicans are going down the path of the cowardly?

Today Trump's approval rating went up bigly while the approval ratings of the mass media and Congress are in the shitter.

If Britain picked up 12 suspects after the June 3, 2017 London attack and then immediately let them go, it is an indication they have no clue what they are up against. Couple that with the fact they had some of the actual terrorists on their radar and let them roam London until the day of doom tells you they are taking the liberals approach to the war on terror.

When you hear of an attack of any kind in a western nation and they refer to the attacker as "Asian" in all probability he is Middle Eastern and that particular country is so obsessed with political correctness they don't protect their citizens' lives properly.

This idea that comedians somehow have an additional level of protection in use of speech is moronic. Are we suppose to believe that comedians are allowed to say what we can't?

Fame whore and former FBI Director James Comey is testifying to nothing this week and is really using the exposure to promote himself and a sure to follow book. Unless he shocks us by saying he is Barack Obama's secret gay lover, then there isn't anything he could say that should be of interest to anyone.

Hillary Clinton has officially demanded a do-over of the election claiming she was robbed. When that came out, Al Gore said he wanted a do-over saying he was robbed.

Former Attorney General Eric Holder aka Mr. Diversity is said to have concluded his investigation into sexual harassment at Uber. Mr. Holder got a bit overzealous and said a man saying good morning to a woman is fine unless he also smiles which shows "Intent to Bang." At that the man is subject to a fine in the form of a donation to the DNC or up to a week of confinement at a conference that has lovely Debbie Wassermann Schultz as the keynote speaker.

Former President Clinton reached out to former President Obama inviting him to fly to Jeffrey Epstein's private island. Obama said only if they have a Turkish bath house.

Radio personality Dennis Prager, former nevertrumper, is urging nevertrump republicans to now support the president. His reasoning is Trump is better than the Left. The problem here is Prager presumes the nevertrump republicans are actually conservatives working on behalf of the voters. This is false, they are working for personal gain and collaborating with wealthy donors to do it. They are the furthest thing from a public servant that you can get. We knew this from observing their behavior during eight years of a destructive presidency under Obama. Republicans have a majority in the House and Senate and we have a republican president. You wouldn't know it.

Former FBI Director James Comey says he was "uneasy" discussing loyalty with Trump. Trump didn't realize in Washington loyalty is something alien to them. They wouldn't know loyalty if it bit them in the butt. It is a town full of back stabbing assholes who are failing the people (see Paul Ryan). Trump now knows this and doesn't expect loyalty from anyone. He was just a naive newcomer who has learned the hard way. At some point in the near future Trump will understand the game and the Washington assholes better be careful because Trump is going to eat them up and spit them out. MAGA.

What's the deal at Fox news with all the horny guys thinking they're Rico Suave.

No wonder Washington didn't want Trump. From the first moment he announced his candidacy, he has exposed all the darkness that politicians use to cloak their activities that have very little to do with the common person and everything to do with them.

I don't care what school they went to if politicians behave as if they have shit for brains it doesn't really matter. And they clown middle America as Podunk, USA. Now that is audacity.

Now liberals are hailing traitors as heroes. I can understand you may not like our current president but now you are showing you don't like our country.

Democratic New York Gov. Andrew Cuomo is talking trash by saying deport me first. What is interesting is there are millions of Americans that would like that since he is a lover of law breakers and essentially a socialist.

Obama's housekeeper Valerie Jarrett has decided to speak out for the Obama shadow government and it is just as stupid as the shit we heard for eight years. Bull shit detectors are going off all over Washington with the epicenter being Obama's new socialist mansion headquarters.

It doesn't really matter how much money he has, George Soros is just a pathetic 86 year old man knocking on Satan's door.

As much as I despise Paul Ryan, and I am a conservative, he is right when he said that Trump is "new to this." Both nevertrump republicans and democrats know this and have used it against Trump and are even trying to find a way to impeach him. So, in essence, we the people have elected an outsider because Washington is so corrupt and the corrupt are using the outsider's lack of protocol, which no one is rushing to school him on, against him. That is the epitome of POS behavior and is indicative of "The Swamp."

FBI officials have announced they recovered a pallet full of Depends. They admit they were used by James Comey for leaking.

If you are standing next to your car and you clearly see all your tires are fully inflated yet a democrat leader is telling you that you are mistaken and one of your tires is flat, are you going to believe them because they must be right or believe what you see right in front of you?

When one observes Sen. Bernie Sanders (D-Head Shop) in a congressional hearing it is clearly obvious that he smokes a blunt before going in. Unfortunately, he must be smoking some bad shit because he turns into an asshole and that is not what Gonga does. I expect him to be laughing with a bag of Cheetos in each hand.

New Sen. Kamala Harris (D-LALA Land) is acting the tough guy and it ain't working. She instead comes off as a majorly rude person. The kind you find in Walmart. Well, she comes from California and the democrat politicians there believe their fecal matter has no scent because they have a super majority. You're not in California anymore, Dorothy.

Al Gore said today that God told him to fight global warming. Not ten minutes later God called and told Gore to shut his pie hole because he is misquoting him and God hates that. What he said is Gore needs to give the globe a break by retiring. God will handle it now.

Valerie Jarrett, former White House nanny, said the "US is no longer a beacon of hope" because of Trump. She suggested Trump could travel the world and trash America thereby validating all the f*cked up countries, spoon with terrorists, cut secret deals to benefit Iran, encourage more boys to become girls and more girls to become boys, screw the Veterans, release a bunch of thugs from prison, bow down to guys with robes and wear a thong. She said all those things worked for Obama.

A gang sweep this morning by the Feds netted 32 democrats. They were booked on charges of Questionable Integrity, Foolishness, Impersonating a Public Servant and Vulgarity.

The only on-street interviews that are legitimate is when you ask the respondent to explain their answer. That is when it becomes obvious they are morons. Example: Do you think it was wise to drop out of the Paris Climate Accord? Answer: No it was stupid and Trump is an idiot. Follow up question: Do you know what the accord is about? Answer: No, not really.

It's true we are all human and share the same planet. The problem is we have a bunch of killers among us who would have us die over an opinion.

Rapper Ice Cube will never rise to the level of a redneck trucker.

Trump ran his own company and the people who worked for him answered to him. Now he is running the country and by rote he handles it like he did his business. How was he to know the f*cked up way Washington operates?

Former President Obama's biggest success (some say only success) was dividing the nation and he did one helluva job. No one can divide a nation like that man. He said he would transform the nation and he did.

Now that the democrats have ruined government policy in all areas, ruined the media and are trying to destroy professional football please don't put them in charge of sex.

You can't understand politics until you live it and breath it. Once you do understand politics you will realize it is a dirty, immoral, unethical and criminal activity. I don't care what intention a politician claims to have going in, once he/she is in they experience a rude awakening. At that point they either bail or stay in there and become one of "them" or they become a renegade like Donald Trump and you can see in real time what he has to contend with. It is fair to compare it to any kind of mafia type association.

So it appears polling aggregator Nate Silver is now the Susan Lucci of polling after the Ossoff loss.

Russia is a bogus argument created by the liberals to defame the conservatives. None of the liberals' accusations are backed up by evidence. What the libtards are doing to Trump is what the conservatives should have done to Obama in 2008/12. This is the payback we get for being civil to Obama who turned out to be nothing more than a failed experiment.

The Daily Caller reported "Hillary told the crowd she was having a hard time getting out of bed and leaving the house." And she said Trump shouldn't be trusted with the nuclear codes. Between Hillary and Biden it's a wonder America still exists.

It might be a good time for Rich Lowry to take another look at Donald Trump's balls. Yeah, those big brass balls Lowry will never have. Those balls got Trump the White House and America another shot at being great again. And by the way Rich, tell your boss Bill Kristol, f*ck you.

Look for Surge 2.0 to happen. The original surge worked great until knickers wearing Obama screwed it up. So look for it to happen again under Trump. Our warriors will be called upon to do what they do best, kill the enemy.

Bankrupt Illinois has asked for contributions from warring gangs.

Let me see if I understand this. Mexicans are marching in the streets of America with a burning American flag and holding the Mexican flag high and carrying signs stating Trump is not our president. What am I missing here? If that is the case, why are they here? No one is forcing them to stay. Are they staying because the entire country of Mexico is a war zone? Are they staying for the free shit they get from American taxpayers? Or are they staying because Mexico's government is even more corrupt than ours? It's probably all of the above. Ingrates all.

If there was a time CNN wasn't fake news it wouldn't have been any better because they're shitty reporters.

Barack Obama threatened to ignore precedent (like that's new) and speak out against Trump when he is a private citizen. No one listens to Obama now. That's why Trump won. In his typical delusional existence, he thinks we will now?

The European Union admitted today that Trump is right and the United States pays 75% of NATO's cost. We certainly don't need NATO to protect America so it makes sense to get its other members to pay their fair share or get another security force. Good luck with that.

Trump won't retain the employee whose job it was to stroke Obama's ego.

When Hillary heard this morning at 8:00 that Trump won't pursue charges she was so happy she continued with her Tequila shooters with a beer back and skipped breakfast. Wait...that was breakfast.

Look at the people who gush over Castro then look at the countries in which government rules either by dictatorship, communism, socialism or religion then explain the gushing. What is wrong with these people? In what way does Castro deserve accolades?

Under the Trump Administration it is hoped the Center For Disease Control will declare political correctness a disease.

You will have to explain to me because I don't understand, how is a cartel member any different than a terrorist? One worships a religion the other worships money. The rest is the same. The two groups should be treated the same militarily. They are a threat to the national security of the United States. It's called a clear and pesent danger.

Don't believe the bad heroin brought in by Mexican Cartels wasn't on purpose. They are killing Americans intentionally.

The Democratic National Committee has decided to change their name to The F*cking Dickheads to more closely resemble their behavior.

Nancy Pelosi said today the Democrat Party is on the side of working class families. Asked if she could identify a particular area of middle class working families that may need attention she mentioned Beverly Hills, Bel Air and Malibu. No mention of Podunk, USA.

The events that have taken place in Turkey with a failed coup and now the assassination of the Russian Ambassador, should point up the danger of having Turkey as an NATO member. Article 5 of the NATO Treaty calls for the protection of a member should they be attacked. Turkey's behaviors invoke attacks.

Democratic Senator Elizabeth Warren is like that crazy aunt who partied too much in the 70's. She can't even talk about the weather without tilting at windmills and shrieking.

In Chicago this Christmas weekend we saw democrats killing each other right and left. Gun controlled Chicago, deemed safe by its mayor Rahm Emanuel, saw 43 shootings and 11 dead to cap off 2016. Now that's progressive!

The way things are progressing, the guy sitting next to you with two days growth on his face and a biker tattoo could very well be named Shirley.

If Qatar is oil rich why does Iran have to fly in food within 48 hours of a six nation blockade led by Saudi Arabia?

A pizza shop owner calls out to his wife the pizza maker and says "Yo, Francine throw some Canadian Bacon and pineapple on that pie for this bozo and the next thing he knows he is crowned the inventor of the Pineapple Pizza. Shouldn't it rightfully go to the bozo who ordered the pie?

Michael Fine, an attorney in Ohio, was jailed for 12 years for hypnotizing clients so he could have sex with them. Didn't Obama hypnotize America and then screwed us for eight years?

This Russian hacking bull shit is a cover up for something that American politicians have done. Whenever you see this kind of behavior it is almost certainly a diversion. And it seems even more so when you see both parties joining together and saying the same thing. Be suspicious or be a fool, the choice is yours.

Many Americans are still having to adjust to it as evidenced by their displeasure with Trump tweeting. What is more transparent than Trump putting it out there raw instead of huddling with staff to come up with a political statement that protects the politician and is typically a lie?

I don't care if you are a democrat, republican, libertarian or a freak of nature (wait...did I already say democrat?) if you think it is okay to jail an illegal immigrant for a crime and when he gets out of prison, despite an order to deport, he isn't deported and commits another crime, you are a moron.

Chelsea Handler won't interview Melania Trump because she "doesn't speak English well." Melania's English is fine as well as the numerous other languages she speaks, whereas Handler only speaks bull shit and doesn't do that very well.

The democrats seem to have so much time on their hands to pursue the Russian hoax and waste our tax dollars that we should have them work part-time. Since they don't actually work they would just "be there" part-time.

As an independent thinker I have always read a cross section of opinions so that I could understand both sides of an issue. The liberals have become so predictable, I don't have to waste time reading their thoughts. It frees me up to do more important things like pick my nose.

Obama is said to be playing a behind-the-scenes role in rebuilding the democratic party he ruined.

A rumor circulated last week that someone in California spotted a republican. After a search was conducted it was determined to be an out-of-towner on vacation asking for directions. California will continue to be an occupied state populated with democrats unless, or until, the state secedes. The republicans gave up on us a long time ago and all we are left with is republican window dressing much like we had with the former governor Arnold Schwarzenegger who used the office and California to polish his image and gain personal wealth.

Elmo was invited to the White House to hopefully mediate a truce between Trump and CNN.

As a conservative I am forced to say the republicans are total assholes for not stepping up for their president. Trump should start a third party. This is just f*cking ridiculous. They should all be thrown out of office and replaced with real republicans.

All this Russia crap would go away if the republicans had balls and weren't f*cking POS traitors. They are harming Trump more than the democrats and they know it and are doing it intentionally. This is why both parties are assholes.

Make no mistake about it, both democrats and republicans are trying to take down Trump because he is an "outsider" upsetting their scam.

Defense Secretary James Mattis has ripped Congress a new asshole because he is shocked at the lack of readiness of our military. We all knew Obama's hatred of the military so my question is where was Graham and McCain and all the other so-called backers of our military? They let this happen and also let happen the VA debacle. And now these POS's are hurting Trump's efforts to fix the mess.

Former basketball star Dennis Rodman is going to North Korea to meet with serial killer Kim Jong-un. He's really doing it to promote his latest venture. As you can see, all the major outlets just gave him free advertising. Let's hope he gets out of North Korea alive.

I voted for Kamala Harris to be a senator from California. Now, after watching her perform in Washington I wouldn't vote for her to clean up my man cave.

An auto parts store owner was confronted with three armed robbers yesterday, the store owner produced his own firearm killing two of the suspects and wounding the third. The police could not release any more information other than the robbers needed more target practice, obviously.

Remember liberals, whenever you are driving through Denver and you feel you need to take a shit, just stop wherever you are and drop your drawers. It's legal now!

Not only has Trump's top aides allowed the fox (Mueller) into the hen house, they are setting the table for his guests (Obama and Hillary supporters).

Virginia Governor Terry McAuliffe (D-Rocket Scientist) held a news conference today after the Scalise shooting and said 93 million people a day are killed by gun violence. That would mean the US would be a vacant lot in less than a week. A confused reporter finally steered him to the right number which he now claims is 93 people a day and 92 of them were in Chicago.

Trump is not stupid, there is a reason why Robert Mueller isn't fired.

Reality Winner (Loser), America's cutest traitor, is said to have turned her portion of prison rec area into a Cross Fit gym. She said after a tough day of being a traitor she likes to wind down with a workout.

Jerry Springer, who has had gutters named after him, had the audacity to say Trump was acting "beneath the dignity of the presidency" when tweeting. Well, if anyone one would know it would be Jerry Springer who exemplifies dignity.

Just in: America has taken out a restraining order against Hillary Clinton. She is not allowed to be within two countries of America.

An elected official in a Mexican border state where a drug cartel is accused of murdering over two hundred people said it was "something that just happened." Of course, how else can it be explained?

Another attack by a person in a van took place in London. And as before, it was described as a white van. Experts are trying to determine why whack jobs prefer white vans while the politically correct are complaining the media is singling out white vans which is racist.

The Indian government is advising pregnant women not to have dirty thoughts. OMG! These are the same people we have entrusted our call centers to.

Scientists have finally discovered the reason why dogs tilt their heads. They do it because they can't believe people can be so stupid. It is a polite way for dogs to say "Are you f*cking kidding me?"

In Michigan, home to the largest concentration of Muslims, a man at the airport screaming Allahu Akbar stabbed a policeman in the neck. The police are not ready to label it a terror attack. Maybe they should ask a fifth grader.

MSNBC's Rachel Maddow was said to have pulled a muscle when reaching for an excuse for the Ossoff loss in Georgia. Something about the weather I think.

True story: Two burglars broke into a home, when the occupant of the home surprised them they bolted towards the door, the burglar in the lead had a gun, the second burglar was carrying a television he dropped while fleeing. I can only assume the guy in the lead thought the sound was the home's occupant shooting at them. The lead guy turns and fires a shot back into the home striking and killing his partner. The police can only report the burglars as having I.Q.'s matching their age.

Fat-ass dictator Kim Jong-un has agreed to halt all nuclear activity on one condition, that the US give him a year's free pass to a buffet of his choice.

There is a bill in Congress but they won't say what it is about or who is working on it. They say it will be passed but won't reveal who will pass it or when it will be passed. When it is passed it will be placed into law but it won't be revealed when. Once it is placed into law, no one will be allowed to know what it is about. Welcome to Congress 2017!

The Venezuelan foreign minister who made the snide remark "Go ahead, send in the Marines" was actually serious I think. Maybe she was hinting they really do want to be saved from the rule of rocket scientist and dancing sensation Nicholas Maduro.

All the Muslims, including the "peaceful" ones, are laughing all the way to our destruction because of all the non-Muslims who are either afraid of their own shadow or have decided the Muslims are to be the top ranked among the oppressed and deserve the most protection. How did it get to this point?

I am not a sci-fi guy but it would be pretty arrogant for us to believe we are the only populated planet in all of the universe. There could be another, more advanced civilization on another planet surveilling us and thinking "What a bunch of idiots" and they wouldn't be speaking of just the democrats.

6/22/2017: Today House Minority Leader Rep. Nancy Pelosi (D-Cuckoo Land) said "she was a "target" because she is "a master legislator." That's like the boxer flat on his back on the mat yelling up to the ref "Dammit, I won this thing."

From Ricky Gervais "What really annoys me is that Trump has convinced his gang that the real enemy is the Hollywood liberal elite." So now we Trump supporters are a gang. If you want to have a civil conversation you don't pepper the other side with vile names. Even a fifth grader knows that.

Rumor has it that NBC is going to sell Megyn Kelly's show to Comedy Central.

Sally Kohn is rumored to be opening a business called Ridiculous Excuses On Demand. The business will be based out of Nancy Pelosi's office.

Despite all the women behind Hillary i.e. Nancy, Debbie, Donna, Maxine, Barack, Meryl, Alyssa, Madonna, etc. they still couldn't get her elected.

World renowned astrophysicist Stephen Hawking wants humanity to leave earth as soon as possible, by Thursday of next week would be good. He said he's outta here tomorrow since he found an Airbnb on Planet Nine.

Gov. Christie, pissed off that his budget wasn't approved shut down public beaches for the 4th of July. Hmm.

Right about now Podunk, USA is feeling brilliant after listening to all the moronic statements from the Trump hating intelligentsia. They sound about as intelligent as my cousin Billy-Bob who lost his two front teeth 27 years ago and figured why the f*ck replace them when he now looks like all the other residents of Podunk.

Researchers using a super computer to simulate what would happen if an asteroid were to approach the earth at a rate of speed equal to thousands of miles per hour, determined we would be in deep shit. Me and my buds figured that out over beer and peanuts in the man cave while Bob was in the crapper.

Mexico was just declared the second most dangerous country in the world behind Syria. Of course, Mexico came out and blamed the drug users in America. If it were not for the terrible American dopers the drug cartels would not exist. And since they do exist it is important that the cartels murder, torture, behead, kidnap, sex traffic and pretty much be people without souls in order to stay in business otherwise what would the poor dopers do? They are providing a public service, after all.

Be patient with Colin Kaepernick. As soon as his girlfriend dumps him and/or his money runs out he will come to his senses. Google his girlfriend and you will understand.

The simple solution to illegal immigration is to not give them what they come here for. We don't even need a wall for that, we need a wall for the criminals and terrorists. If we don't give illegals jobs, welfare and freedom, they won't come. At some point Mexicans are going to have to demand their government fix their country. It is a small number of people holding the country back. They must go.

The Pentagon said it spent $30 million on the wrong colored uniform for the Afghan Army. That I don't care about, what I care about is we spent $30 million on their uniforms to begin with. The Afghans can sell some f*cking oil and buy the uniforms themselves.

Apartment management informed a 20 year old female tenant she would have to leave the pool area because she was wearing a bathing suit that would excite teenage boys. If the sun comes up in the morning or the wind blows it excites teenage boys.

A former dominatrix turned rookie cop in New Jersey is awaiting a decision on if she will keep her job after her former occupation was discovered. It will depend on a psychiatric interview to determine if she would be prone to excessive force. Meanwhile, a petition signed by thousands of local criminals are demanding she keep her new job and they are ready to be arrested.

New democratic senator from the commune of California Kamala Harris is off to a fast and vocal start. Not sure if being a younger version of Maxine Waters is a good strategy.

Yesterday, in the middle of the afternoon while hearing a case, Supreme Court Justice Ruth Ginsburg retired. We found out later she just retired for her afternoon nap.

While the House GOP is saying Supreme Court Justice Ruth Ginsburg should recuse herself from ruling on Trump's travel ban because she spoke out against it publicly, Trump supporters are demanding she recuse herself from the Supreme Court.

Crooks are crooks. Everyone knows this. They come in the form of billionaires, corporations and high level politicians not just the thug in the street. The thug in the street is near harmless compared to the "high class" aforementioned thugs. But the only reason these thugs can exist is if we allow it. We meaning the commoner. If we swallow what they feed us without asking what it is, we have given them permission to do whatever. What the democrats and republicans are doing right now to make our lives miserable, we allow and we can stop.

I live in California. The only people who are allowed to carry firearms concealed are the criminals.

Does anyone see the irony in the United States government, both democrats and republicans, chastising Russia for interfering in another country's elections including ours? We perfected that strategy.

Director and activist Michael Moore is donating $10,000 to New York City's Shakespeare in the Park. This after donating $10,000 to buffets the last two weeks which didn't allow him to be very active.

What is happening to ESPN? First their sportscasters all go to the left politically and talk more politics than sports, now they are featuring naked male athletes.

MSNBC commentator Donny Douche said today he is "going to go thug" he is so pissed at Trump. He said for Trump to meet him "in the schoolyard." This would be in the schoolyard of some prestigious school I imagine because Douche wouldn't dare go in the neighborhood. He's so pretty they would beat his ass and then cornhole him. Donny would be more threatening in a romper and with a man bun.